CULTURAL JOURNEYS IN
HIGHER EDUCATION

Great Debates in Higher Education is a series of short, accessible books addressing key challenges to and issues in higher education, on a national and international level. These books are research-informed but debate-driven. They are intended to be relevant to a broad spectrum of researchers, students and administrators in higher education and are designed to help us unpick and assess the state of higher education systems, policies and social and economic impacts.

Published titles:

British Universities in the Brexit Moment: Political, Economic and Cultural Implications
Mike Finn

Sexual Violence on Campus: Power-Conscious Approaches to Awareness, Prevention, and Response
Chris Linder

Higher Education, Access and Funding: The UK in International Perspective
Edited by Sheila Riddell, Sarah Minty, Elisabet Weedon, and Susan Whittaker

Evaluating Scholarship and Research Impact: History, Practices, and Policy Development
Jeffrey W. Alstete, Nicholas J. Beutell, and John P. Meyer

Access to Success and Social Mobility through Higher Education: A Curate's Egg?
Edited by Stuart Billingham

The Marketisation of English Higher Education: A Policy Analysis of a Risk-based System
Colin McCaig

Refugees in Higher Education: Debate, Discourse and Practice
Jacqueline Stevenson and Sally Baker

Radicalisation and Counter-Radicalisation in Higher Education
Catherine McGlynn and Shaun McDaid

Forthcoming titles:

Dissent in the Neoliberal University
Sean Sturm and Steven Turner

Degendering Leadership in Higher Education
Barret Katuna

Class, Gender, Race and the Teaching Excellence Framework:
Diversity Deficits in Higher Education Evaluations
Amanda French and Kate Carruthers Thomas

Academic Leadership and Management in the UK: The View
from the Middle
Jane Creaton and Peter Starie

CULTURAL JOURNEYS IN HIGHER EDUCATION

Student Voices and Narratives

BY

JAN BAMFORD
London Metropolitan University

LUCIE POLLARD
University of the West of Scotland

United Kingdom — North America — Japan
India — Malaysia — China

Emerald Publishing Limited
Howard House, Wagon Lane, Bingley BD16 1WA, UK

First edition 2019

British Library Cataloguing in Publication Data
A catalogue record for this book is available from the British
Library

ISBN: 978-1-78743-859-0 (Print)
ISBN: 978-1-78743-858-3 (Online)
ISBN: 978-1-78743-995-5 (Epub)

ISOQAR certified
Management System,
awarded to Emerald
for adherence to
Environmental
standard
ISO 14001:2004.

Certificate Number 1985
ISO 14001

INVESTOR IN PEOPLE

CONTENTS

Preface   ix

Acknowledgements   xiii

Introduction   1

1. Bridging Barriers   11

2. Strangers in a New Land   25

3. 'Leaving Culture at the Classroom Door'   49

4. Strangers in Your Own Land   75

5. Culture and Developing Relationality in
    Higher Education   105

Bibliography   125

Index   143

PREFACE

Understanding culture is, as Geertz suggests, the interpretation of individuals' stories about their cultural interactions and activities. The story allows for a 'metasocial commentary' of the participants within 'a story they tell themselves about themselves' (Geertz, 1974, p. 448).

This interpretation of culture by Clifford Geertz frames for us the journey that the reader will take in reading this book. Culture frames our existence, our lives and our learning. In writing this book, we have drawn not only on our collective years of working in higher education but also on our own cultural identities, in terms of family background and cultural interactions throughout our lives. These experiences have informed our world view and have been the genesis for this book.

We have previously known and supported students from both a typical UK background and those who come to university from different cultures, whether that is from a UK base or indeed arriving in the United Kingdom from the country where they grew up. We have witnessed increasingly culturally diverse classrooms which bring challenges to communication amongst different student groups and between students and their lecturers. The importance of understanding communication patterns and how to communicate across different groups is given a lot of attention in the business world but as yet, there still appears to be insufficient acknowledgement within higher education of the importance of differing communication patterns and the impact that this can have on the education process. Our observations of student interactions over the years led us to explore in more detail the impact of these differing communication patterns from the students' perspectives. We have framed these communications in a relationship discourse because that is the way that they appear to impact on cultural identity and on the learning processes.

We were inspired by the narratives of students in our previous research, which we have drawn on to frame the discussion in our first chapter, to delve further work into understanding the experiences, struggles and barriers that students face throughout their time in higher education. We believe that more attention should be given to the complex issues that arise around cultural communication in the classroom and around the impact of cultural interactions as part of the learning process. There is certainly more discussion to be had with regard to the existential and ontological aspects of the higher education process. This book sits firmly within the existential in terms of its parameters because of its focus on relationships and the link between relationships and learning in a cultural context. It is not a philosophical work, and we have not attempted to enter into a philosophical discussion or a discussion about multiculturalism, migrants and global cultural shifts; instead, we have focused on the students' experience of their higher education in a cultural context and via their own recounting of their cultural journeys.

Students wanted us to give voice to the conversations that we had as they felt passionately about being heard and sometimes felt they were silenced and ignored. It is this expression of passion in the desire to be heard, to have their stories told that formed the approach for this book. In using their words to retell their stories, sometimes, the grammar is incorrect or there is a use of slang expression. We draw the reader's attention to this so that a clearer understanding of the aims and objectives of this work is achieved. The stories are sometimes challenging to read and sometimes make for uncomfortable reading. We have repeated these uncomfortable sections of students' narratives both for impact and to ensure that we have presented their stories in a way that is as true a representation as possible. Inevitably, we recognise that perceptions are just that and are situated in a particular time and place. The perceptions are important, however, in understanding the 'lived reality' of our higher education experience for students. The narratives therefore cannot be viewed as one dimensional and are framed by time and space and location on a number of levels.

We feel that the stories that have been repeated in this book are powerful and point to a need for change. A view that universities need to shift in their approach in aiding students to achieve their best in increasingly culturally diverse classrooms. Higher education is ideally placed to affect changes and shine a light on the lived reality through the voices of the participants in this book and their cultural journeys. The stories that have been retold here highlight the ways in the multitude of deeply held beliefs, values, behaviours, traditions and approaches to others inform the journey of each individual in this book. These complexities allow us to nether into their world in their words.

ACKNOWLEDGEMENTS

In addition, we owe our very deepest debt of gratitude to our interviewees and our students without whom this work would not have been possible and who generously gave of their free time to tell us about their cultural journeys. We hope that the contents provide faithful representations of your cultural journeys and truly reflect your stories. Any errors or omissions may be laid fully at our door!

To our families for their loving help, kindness, support and advice on this journey and to our colleagues for talking through our ideas and to all those who patiently sat through our conference presentations and those whom we bored with our discussion of our views on cultural identity and students' higher education experiences. We would also like to thank Clare for her helpful comments on reading through our drafts and to all those colleagues who have offered words of encouragement along the way — thank you for bearing with us as it seemed to take a long time. A particular thank you goes to Kimberley at Emerald Publishing for her patience during various delays to our final draft.

INTRODUCTION

Throughout our time working in higher education, we continue to be struck by the importance of understanding and listening to students who enter our university systems. A shared interest in the cultural diversity of the higher education environment is what drew us to embark on this research journey. The value of recognising the student perspective was reinforced by research that we undertook in 2012 on student engagement in culturally diverse classrooms (Bamford, Djebbour, & Pollard, 2015; Bamford & Pollard, 2018). This research formed the basis for developing this book as we were struck by the number of home students[1] who reported that English was not the language spoken at home and the seeming lack of communication across what we define as different cultural groups. Perhaps this should not have come as a surprise to us, but it gave us an opportunity to reflect on our own assumptions and our teaching practices, together with the cultural encounters these students have and the challenges that may arise as a consequence.

In writing this book, we hope to provide readers with a unique and as yet hidden insight into students' perspectives of their higher education experience in the United Kingdom; the trials that they encounter; and the skills they use in negotiating their way through higher education. We have taken the view that the narratives recounted by the students in this book represent journeys which are unique to each individual but which also demonstrate some commonality amongst the barriers and benefits that the students described. Our writing has been informed not only by the research data we collected for this book but also by our combined research experience of students' cultural interactions and the importance of such interactions in navigating higher education in this country, particularly for those studying in urban universities. Whilst we acknowledge the limitations of such an approach, we believe the insights that we provide outweigh the methodological challenges and limitations of space.

This chapter provides the context for the reasons we have chosen to undertake this research. It gives voice to a project that explored and analysed the cultural interactions of students in the context of a journey that they have embarked on and which has at its centre the higher education learning experience. It is our view that, despite the plethora of research on international students and their experiences, little work has been undertaken that explores first-, second- and third-generation migrant experiences together with the challenges and barriers they face. In giving a voice to these students' cultural journeys, we hope to provide a clearer understanding of the importance of relationships and culture to the higher education learning environment.

Our previously Higher Education Academy (HEA) funded research project demonstrated to us that there was the need for more qualitative and in-depth exploration of the students' voices with regard to their higher education experience. This project surveyed over 390 students in two post-92 institutions[2] in London. The student demographics were similar at each institution and can be viewed as typical for an urban higher education institution (HEI). What was striking to us was that of the 56.3% of respondents who identified themselves as home students, 70.3% had parents who were not born in the United Kingdom and 48.3% of all respondents identified that they were non-native speakers of English. In addition, 43.9% identified themselves as European students (Bamford et al., 2015; Bamford & Pollard, 2018). Data from the HEA project provided us with further context and contributed to the themes that we identify in subsequent chapters. Our findings highlight the need to hear more from the individuals themselves, their lived experience and the way in which the phenomenon of individuals' cultural backgrounds formed part of their educational journey.

1.1. THE CULTURAL CLASSROOM

In 2016/2017, there were just over 2.3 million people studying at UK HEIs (HESA, 2018). As the make-up of the UK population changes, there are increasing numbers of students either whose parents or grandparents immigrated to the United Kingdom or who are recent immigrants themselves. For those students where English is not the language spoken at home, and where there is less congruency between their home culture and that found within the UK academic settings, there appears to be a greater requirement to support their transition into university (Bamford et al., 2015). This need is heightened where, as many of them are, these students are the first generation in their family to embark on a journey into higher education.

When we refer to 'culture' in this book, we reference it in its broadest sense and have found McNamee and Faulkner's definition of culture useful:

> [...] norms, roles, values, beliefs, rituals, traditions –
> represents the boundary between members and

> *non-members. Culture provides what one needs to know to function as a member in good standing within various groups to which the person belongs. Culture gives one both a way to make sense of the world and an orientation to it. It represents a set of assumptions about how the world works and how people within the group are expected to relate to one another. Culture includes guidelines for acceptable behaviour, including appropriate gestures, words, tones and demeanour expected in rituals of greeting, eating and meeting and so on.*
> *(McNamee & Faulkner, 2001, p. 67)*

Understanding modes of 'acceptable behaviour' (including gestures, tone, words and demeanour) is important in framing students' interaction in the culturally diverse classrooms of contemporary HE. Hence, this leads us to viewing classroom interactions as culturally and relationally steeped (Bamford & Pollard, 2018). This is further informed by Clifford Geertz' (1973) view that culture is the fabric of meaning for individuals.

The focus in the current literature is predominantly on Black and Asian Ethnic Minority (BAME) students' attainment, and this literature has provided the backdrop to our research. The tapestry of the current debate is centred around the differential outcomes data for these students. In addition, the issue of culture in the classroom is discussed in the current literature, predominantly within the context of the international student experience and not in relation to BAME students. Where is the cultural discussion of those who come from diverse backgrounds but who are not defined as 'international' by universities? Despite this lack of recognition, Black and Asian students are more likely to apply to universities than they did in previous years (UCAS, 2017). Research suggests that these students tend to fare less well than their white counterparts, irrespective of entry qualifications, age and academic provider (Dent, 2017; Miller, 2016; Mountford-Zimdars, Sanders, Jones, Sabri, & Moore, 2015). Another dynamic is that the students who are the focus of this book tend to come from lower socio-economic groups and are often the first in their family to attend university. There is a wealth of research that suggests that these socio-economic differences have a role to play in student attainment. Students from the most deprived socio-economic groups are more likely to leave university within two years, less likely to complete their degrees within five years and less likely to graduate with a first-class honours degree or a 2:1 (Crawford, 2014; Mountford-Zimdars et al., 2015).

What if student attainment in itself is culturally defined? In essence, do we as academics tend to view culture from the perspective of our own culturally defined framework and rarely see the world through the eyes of those from other cultures? As we think and dream in our native language, it is difficult to have an understanding of the deep-seated cultural behaviours of other cultures in which another language is the basis for communication. This standpoint affects multiple levels of reality, and awareness of the challenge is the first step to understand the viewpoint of those who have differing cultural norms, rules and values. For example, Rowntree, Zufferey, and King (2016) argue that Western concepts of attainment are based solely on high academic performance and grade outcome; yet attainment for many students is simply being able to integrate well into university life. For international students, this may include adapting to host societies (Grayson, 2008), while for other groups of students, it may simply be about gaining an understanding of the 'higher education culture' (Bamford et al., 2015). These differences may in part explain why, in spite of the clearly articulated commitments that UK universities make to diversity and inclusion, these have not yet been translated into equality of opportunity, a concern that some attribute to the teaching and learning experiences encountered (Mountford-Zimdars et al., 2017). This might suggest that universities focus too heavily on academic outcomes, ignoring the more nuanced aspects of university life, the class-cultural discontinuities, the relationality between students and the importance of 'feeling university' (Bamford et al., 2015; Bamford & Pollard, 2018; Lehmann, 2007).

Clearly, the reasons for the differences in experience and attainment are complex and are challenging to pinpoint in terms of single points of action. Do students from lower socio-economic backgrounds have less social capital, or is it simply that they have external pressures that hinder their academic achievement? (Crawford, 2014; Jones, 2017) However, students from higher socio-economic backgrounds may have better adaption skills and may be more resilient: or are they simply better at integrating into the university culture and at fitting in (Jury et al., 2017)?

I.2. METHODOLOGY

In an attempt to address these questions, we designed a research approach that would retell the students' experiences and their journeys in higher education, thereby understanding the 'lived experiences' from the perspective of those that have transitioned into higher education.

A narrative approach was chosen as it was felt that this would provide a stronger appreciation of the students' lived experiences: an approach that Goodson and Sikes (2001) define as 'learning from lives'. This narrative-telling allowed us to gain an understanding of the students' past and present, together with how relationships and the overcoming of challenges impacted on their academic success. Story-telling is part of the fabric of human lives, bringing meaning to experiences and supporting the concept of community. A narrative approach gives voice to the journeys these students had been on and provides us with insights into how their lives have been shaped and how they interpret their lives through the telling of stories (Clandinin & Huber, 2005).

As Roland Barthes reminds us:

> *Narrative is present in myth, legend, fable, tale,*
> *novella, epic, history, tragedy, drama, comedy,*
> *mime, painting (think of Carpaccio's Saint Ursula),*
> *stained-glass windows, cinema, comics, news items,*
> *conversation. Moreover, under this almost infinite*
> *diversity of forms, narrative is present in every age,*
> *in every place, in every society; it begins with the*
> *very history of mankind and there nowhere is nor*
> *has been a people without narrative [...] Caring*
> *nothing for the division between good and bad*
> *literature, narrative is international, trans historical,*
> *transcultural: it is simply there, like life itself.*
> *(1993, pp. 251–252)*

The narrative interview has been accepted as a qualitative research method for over 40 years (Clandinin & Caine, 2008). Narrative inquiry can focus on a single event or series of events. In our study, face-to-face biographical narrative interviews were conducted with 20 students from eight HEIs. They included both post-92 and Russell Group universities which were located either in London or in the North of England. Interviewees recalled not only their educational journeys that took them to university but also their transition and persistence at university.

Male and female students were self-selecting through open requests, facilitated by academic staff, and came from a range of socio-demographic, religious and ethnic groups. Using the frameworks of Jovchelovitch and Bauer (2000), unstructured in-depth interviews were utilised with selected themes and topics. These interviews allowed for an in-depth exploration of the students' journeys, the key moments in that journey, as well as their perceptions and experiences to date. They sought to learn about the adaption that individual students made throughout that journey, the cultural interactions that took place, the challenges faced inside and outside the classroom and the potential benefits that arose from these interactions. We sought to understand the complexity of the interactions that students had with others, and how they perceived themselves and their peers, that is, their agency. We also learnt through the process the importance of family: family background and the value that family placed on the education they were receiving.

It is recognised that a major limitation of this approach is that we as researchers interpret the narrative, shaping it and retelling it through our perceived standpoint. There is a risk that the stories we are narrating are recounted in a selective way in as much that what we share with the reader may only be a small part of the conversations that we have heard. However, Clandinin and Huber (2005) warn of the dangers of coding data as this opposes the very concept of narration. Therefore, in our analysis, we have attempted to ensure that the interviewees' cultural and institutional points of reference are dominant. In order to give voice to the experiences, the words are theirs and we have chosen to present lengthy excerpts, retold verbatim, from the narratives to allow the reader to hear directly from the students. Perception and memory are not stationary and the lens through which they are recounted is limited by those perceptions and time constraints. They were formed by a particular view at a particular time. We make this observation both in terms of the above and in terms of the limitation of how a person views themselves in a situated context. This view may be governed by mood, for example, at that particular point in time. Therefore, they provide situated insights and not a continuation of experience. The stories are corroborated by the previous research we have undertaken, by our own experiences of working with students in London institutions over a period of many years and in the way in which the themes that we identified presented a unified picture. The reading and rereading of the narratives independently and together strengthened our interpretive approach and the reliability of the data.

The ethical considerations that surround the use of narrative inquiry are well documented (Clandinin & Huber, 2005). We have remained cognisant of the importance of relationality and the need for fidelity to the relationships the participants had with other students, academics and with us, as researchers, throughout. In narrative inquiry, researchers need to acknowledge the confidences shared within the relationship between the interviewer and interviewee and ensure that they do not interpret the narratives to ensure the true voice of the narrator comes through.

Ethical approval was sought and obtained in accordance with British Education Research Association (BERA) guidelines (2011). All participants voluntarily provided informed consent; the study information provided was clear and informed participants of the objectives of the study. All participants understood that they had the right to withdraw at any time and were guaranteed confidentiality. To maintain the interviewees' anonymity, real names have been replaced with pseudonyms.

NOTES

1. Home students are defined as those that are UK nationals.

2. Post-92 Institutions refer to UK institutions (often former polytechnics) that were granted university status through the Further and Higher Education Act 1992.

CHAPTER 1

BRIDGING BARRIERS

From our earlier research and the stories that we heard, themes of resiliency, belonging and the shaping and reshaping of community emerged. We will explore these ideas in the subsequent chapters. This first chapter sets out a context for our research and revisits some of our earlier work.

Our previously published work drew on data from a survey of students from two post-1992 institutions in London (Bamford & Pollard, 2018; Bamford et al., 2015; Bamford, Djebbour, & Pollard, 2014). We found that there were significant challenges with regard to communication across different cultural groups and that the number of students identifying as non-native speakers was surprisingly high for what had been perceived to be a 'home' student population. The demographics of the students surveyed in this data were similar at the two post-1992 institutions' research sites. The largest cultural grouping was one where students identified themselves as white: this amounted to 54.5% of respondents. The next largest group was Asian with 17.5%, while 15% of respondents identified themselves as Black. Of the 56.3% of respondents who identified themselves as neither European nor international students, 70.3% had parents who were born outside the United Kingdom and 48.3% of all respondents identified that they were non-native speakers of English. In addition, 43.9% identified themselves as European students. These findings led us to explore the impact of such culturally diverse cohorts from the students' perspectives in more depth. The survey instrument was an adapted version of the US National Survey on Student Engagement (NSSE),[1] and Table 1.1 provides a list of the engagement items which we found were useful indicators on key issues relating to student engagement. The items also helped us to identify the lack of communication and relationship building amongst students. We found significant differences with regard to students' communication with each other and with their lecturers, and between those who were native and the non-native speakers of English (Bamford et al., 2015).

As outlined in the introduction, we wanted to hear more from individuals studying in UK higher education about their lived experience and the way in which the phenomenon of individuals' cultural backgrounds shaped their educational journey. The NSSE research pointed to questions of 'resiliency' and 'belonging' which are explored in the remainder of this chapter. Although there is much interlinkage between the two themes, they are discussed separately and provide a clearer understanding of the challenges that universities and their diverse student bodies face.

1.1. RESILIENCY

We have viewed the concept of resilience using the definition offered by Liebenberg, Ungar, and Vijver (2012, p. 219) as: 'the capacity of individuals to overcome adversity and do well in spite of exposure to significant adversity'. We do this largely because this definition resonates well with our

Table 1.1. Engagement Items from the NSSE.

Item	Statement
E1	Asked questions in class or contributed to class discussions
E2	Made a class presentation
E3	Prepared two or more drafts of a chapter or assignment before turning it in
E4	Worked on a chapter or project that required integrating ideas or information from various sources
E5	Included diverse perspectives (different races, religions, genders, political beliefs, etc.) in class discussions or writing assignments
E6	Came to class without completing readings or assignments during class
E7	Worked with other students on projects during class
E8	Worked with classmates outside of class to prepare class assignments
E9	Put together ideas or concepts from different courses when completing assignments or during class discussions
E10	Explained course material to one or more students
E11	Participated in a community-based project (e.g. service learning) as part of a regular course
E12	Used an electronic medium (chat group, Internet, instant messaging, etc.) to discuss or complete an assignment
E13	Used email to communicate with a lecturer
E14	Discussed grades or assignments with a lecturer
E15	Talked about career plans with an academic tutor
E16	Discussed ideas from your readings or classes with faculty members outside of class
E17	Worked harder that you thought you could to meet a lecturer's standards or expectations
E18	Worked with faculty members on activities other than coursework (committees, orientation, student life activities, etc.)

Table 1.1. *(Continued)*

Item	Statement
E19	Discussed ideas from your readings or classes with others outside of class (student, family members, co-workers etc.)
E20	Had serious conversations with students of a different race or ethnicity that your own
E21	Had serious conversations with students who are different from you in terms of their religious beliefs, political opinions or personal values

students' stories. The sense of resourcefulness, adaptation to challenges and supporting a sense of well-being are aspects that have been described by Cassidy (2015). Our research has shown that resilience in students from different cultural backgrounds is borne through the development of protective factors and the adoption of coping skills, for example self-efficacy, building of networks and engagement, thus enabling students to cope with the changing dynamics that they face in their academic journey (Bamford et al., 2015).

The transition to university is, for most young adults, one of the most tumultuous events of their lives, and universities are being challenged to do more to recognise the issues and to offer more support. In September 2017, a survey in *The Guardian* newspaper on student satisfaction reported that 87% of first-year students found it difficult to cope with the academic and social aspects of university life, and many reported that they found the transition from home to university as a source of considerable stress (Wakeford, 2017).

At a time when five times more students are reporting mental health issues then they did 10 years ago (BBC News,

2017), universities need to look at ways to help students build resilience. Joanna Mills (BERA Blog, 2015) suggests that while some students demonstrate social competence through effective communication and acceptance of others and other people's views, many young adults do not. She believes that universities should look to offer more role-play, project-based learning together with exposure to industry to build social competence. We too found that there was greater relationality when students were engaged in more experiential learning through role-play (Bamford et al., 2014).

The term 'academic resilience' describes the characteristics of students who remain motivated and perform well in spite of the difficulties that they may encounter (Cassidy, 2015). A sense of 'grit' and 'mindset' that Duckworth, Peterson, Matthews, and Kelly (2007) depict so well, and is echoed throughout our research, is evident for one student, Maria, as she describes her own experiences:

> *I've sometimes got struggling times, but I choose to do this, because I want to do it! And I'll do it no matter if I have to fight the world if I have to! But it's my drive.*

Students' stories helped us realise that this ability to thrive, adapt and cope with stress are important attributes not only of their transition into university but also of their continued academic success (Bamford et al., 2015). This is thrown into particularly sharp focus when cultural differences are an aspect of the transition to university. Our findings echo those of others who have shown that high levels of resilience promote positive student performance and outcomes (Cassidy, 2015; Chung & Turnbull, 2017).

Our research examined the development of resilience as students progress through their studies and found that there was a significant difference between their engagement and communication in their first year of study compared to their final year. Our results therefore support the premise that the development of resilience is an important aspect of the learning process and supports academic progression. We also found that native and non-native speakers of English differ in their resilience. For example, a notable difference that we observed was their behaviour with respect to their communication with the lecturer or especially when talking about career plans with an academic tutor. It was apparent that non-native students were significantly worse off in terms of their alienation from their fellow students and their studies.

However, we found particularly for non-natives speakers, there were gains over the three years, including diverse perspectives in work,[2] collaborating with classmates outside class and putting together ideas from different courses. Therefore, non-native speakers may cope by becoming more creative and by discussing the work with classmates, thus reinforcing the importance of relationality that we explore in later chapters. It is interesting to note that when asked what represents the quality of relationships with people at the institution, respondents ranked their relationships with other students the highest: fellow students were ranked as 'friendly', 'helpful' and 'supportive' by 63% of respondents, compared to 53% for lecturers and 33% for administrative staff, thus underlining the importance of the students' communities of practice. The seemingly negative perception of the administrative support and the need to navigate unfamiliar rules are evidenced throughout the interviews with students.

Factors that contribute to resilience have been identified by Gunnestad (2006) as:

- external network factors (e.g. support from families and friends);

- internal factors (the individuals' abilities and skills); and

- existential factors such as meaning, values and faith.

This third factor links the issue of resilience and the cultural identity of students. We have previously proposed that culture pervades all factors, and students from different cultures can draw on resilience traits to help them adjust to the new environments (Bamford et al., 2015). One of the questions that we felt we wanted to address was whether the cultural capital students bring with them helps to develop their resilience and can we, as educators, channel this to support their academic growth? Crisp, Taggart, and Nora (2015) observed that, in their study, Latina/Latino university students drew on their cultural knowledge to build resilience and support their academic success.

Glass and Westmont's resilience-based model (Glass & Westmont, 2014) highlights the positive impact of belonging and social interaction on stress, together with students' ability to overcome academic and external barriers to learning. Similar to these studies, our research highlighted the need for students to feel that they are in a supportive academic environment that encourages engagement and that enables them to participate in community activities (Bamford et al., 2015; Wang, Walberg, & Haertel, 1994). The importance of the factors identified by Gunnestad in terms of networks, values and meaning links to concepts that we have identified with a sense of belonging in higher education (Bamford et al., 2015).

1.2. BELONGING

The need to belong is one of the most prevailing motivators of human social behaviour. It is an innate need that, if threatened, can lead to poor self-belief and diminished cognitive function (Lewis, Stout, Pollock, Finkelstein, & Ito, 2016; Osterman, 2000). Goodenow (1993, p. 80) suggests that a sense of belonging reflects 'the extent to which students feel personally accepted, respected, included, and supported by others in the school social environment'. Belonging has been shown to be linked to social capital (i.e. resources generated by our relationship with others) and to an individual's happiness (Soria & Stebleton, 2013).

Our previous research (Bamford & Pollard, 2018; Bamford et al., 2015) has underlined that the sense of student belonging is fundamental to the learning experience. It contributes to the need of students to feel valued and to feel accepted not only by the institution but also by their student peers. This desire to belong is observed even before students arrive at university, with Black, Asian and Minority Ethnic (BAME) students preferentially selecting post-1992, inner-city universities (HESA, 2018; Miller, 2016). The reasons for this preference are no doubt complex but we can surmise that perhaps these universities are closer to home, thereby enabling students to commute to university and remain living with family.[3] These universities may also be perceived as less elitist and more inclusive, than, for example, Russell Group universities.

This sense of belonging is increasingly a focus of research in higher education, with the importance of nurturing a culture of belonging being emphasised (Thomas, 2012; Trowler, 2010). The idea of not fitting in is often cited as a reason for poor academic attainment amongst ethnic minority students (Mountford-Zimdars et al., 2015). However, the reasons why these students find it hard to fit in are not easily identified, although social and cultural biases within the classroom may be partly to blame.

This notion of bias is described by Thomas (2002) within the context of *the institutional habitus*, where the institutions' attributes and behaviours need to be negotiated by the student and that this mediation is influenced by class, gender and culture (Reay, 2004). The extent to which culture impedes this negotiation of the higher education landscape has been previously examined (Welikala & Watkins, 2008; Zepke & Leach, 2005). Zepke and Leach believe that 'higher education is seen through a distinctive lens shaped from a Western cultural and epistemological perspective' and that because of this, 'some students withdraw before achieving their original goals' (Zepke & Leach, 2005, p. 55).

Although Welikala and Watkins' (2008) work on cultural scripts focused on international students, their ideas easily translate to all students within the culturally heterogeneous classroom of contemporary UK higher education. Students will find it less easy to fit in if they are not adept at reading normative communication cues. As they transition into university, they will inevitably find that their frames of reference are discordant with the new experiences they are facing.

1.3. HOW CAN INSTITUTIONS SUPPORT A SENSE OF BELONGING?

How then can we facilitate the building of belonging, thereby supporting those whose cultural background is perhaps not in tune with the *habitus* of the higher education environment?

Building a sense of belonging has often been discussed in relation to student engagement (Masika & Jones, 2016; Thomas, 2012; Trowler, 2010). Kahu (2013) has identified that participation (and therefore engagement) in the classroom, with both academic staff and peers, is strongly indicative of a sense of belonging. Tinto's model of learning proposes that academic success is linked to both formal engagement (with the curriculum and with academics) and informal engagement (with peers and with social events)

(Tinto, 1987). Tinto's work suggests that students need to engage in both systems to succeed and progress. Interestingly, when lecturers talk about their own academic struggles, students better appreciate the difficulties of fitting in. Through these narratives, they are able to gain a sense of belonging, and 'buy in' to university life, which, in turn, promotes social and cultural capital and helps build their own self-efficacy (Morales, 2014; Zepke & Leach, 2005).

Traditionally, immigrants are expected to assimilate – where integration into our education systems is key to social assimilation (Dronkers & Fleischmann, 2010). There is a body of evidence that supports the view that academic and social engagement facilitates integration/acculturation into higher education and, in turn, provides academic and learning gains (Pike & Kuh, 2005; Thomas, 2012; Yorke, 2016). Pike and Kuh (2005) looked at the success and integration of first-generation students at university (i.e. those whose parents had not attended tertiary education) and found that these students tended to be from lower socio-economic groups; they found it harder to be acculturated into the new behaviours and language that are 'university'. These students are less likely to form social groups and lower levels of engagement are often observed.

In spite of the importance of social interaction and better transition in the context of education resilience, there is insufficient focus on cultural transition and the need to support engagement. This is supported by the findings of Cherng, Turney, and Kao (2014) who have shown that minority groups and students who are first- and second-generation secondary students in the United States are less likely to engage in extracurricular activities and therefore have a reduced likelihood to form the social interactions that support transition into tertiary education. This intercultural dimension presents not only a challenge but also a learning opportunity. Caruana

(2014) argues that the current intercultural dimension of the internationalised university requires a pedagogy of 'cosmopolitanism'. Her research describes students' struggles in the unfamiliar culture of university, the lack of community and the associated support mechanisms within that community (e.g. familiar traditions, faith and family values that all provide individuals with meaning).

Interestingly, there is little research into the concept of student transition as cultural adaptation. Yet as early as 1987, the work of Tinto emphasised the importance of student interaction and their integration into the university. His work revealed that the way in which students adjusted to academic life was very much related to their social background and the 'fit' of university.

Reference to the socio-cultural theories of learning is important here, where student participation in social interactions develops autonomous thinking and problem-solving skills. Lave (1993) states that learning that leads to autonomy and a fuller community life cannot be identified in terms of single identifiable tools such as assigned tasks, but it lies in the relations amongst individuals, where the social interactions between students are viewed as a key part of the learning process.

Interactions with staff and peers seem to be especially important when cultural differences are at work, particularly for those students with little or no understanding or experience of UK higher education at home to draw upon (Read, Archer, & Leathwood, 2003). The ideas are supported by the work of Meeuwisse, Born, and Severiens (2010), who found that for students from minority ethnic backgrounds and for those who are first generation in higher education, it was the quality of the interactions that was strongly indicative of academic progress and success.

In the current higher education environment, where the cultural make-up of institutions' student bodies is increasingly diverse, the need for universities to adapt and build social cohesion has probably never been so great.

There is a perception from the students we spoke to that academics all too often view student engagement as the responsibility of the student and that the student needs to be an active learner and interact within the classroom. Very few of the academics we encountered believed that they, or their institution, had a role to play in developing engaged learners. This implies that students are inert or apathetic but we have argued that student engagement must be viewed through a lens of cultural transition and that the onus is jointly held by students and the institution.

This is supported by our earlier interviews with students (Bamford et al., 2015) who conveyed a sense of disappointment that their institutions did not do more to support them and encourage engagement across the different cultural groups:

> *Student 1: [...] I think that they don't really accommodate different cultural social events in universities in England because I for example have a friend [...] she is not drinking alcohol due to religious reasons [...] We sit down and drink coffee together.*

> *Student 2: I don't think that university offers you that interaction with students from different countries on a different level than the actual class itself. You are forced to work with people [...] you are forced [...] you have to work with people in groups. That group work for me is a disaster!*

These comments appear to reinforce the notion of distancing, together with a lack of effective communication amongst student groups. This links to issues of belonging, engagement and cultural dissonance, aspects of the student experience that are explored further in Chapter 4.

Zepke and Leach (2005) identify that engagement cannot be assumed because students come to university with a myriad of other commitments, for example caring responsibilities, or part-time work. This puts the onus on the institution to adapt to the students' needs, and to fit the university around the students' lives and not the other way around. Kahu (2013) explains that engagement can be regarded both as instrumental (task-orientated) and as intuitive (enjoyment-orientated). She also discusses a third aspect of conation – the will to succeed. We too, in our research, have identified the importance of a will to learn (Bamford et al., 2015), and the figures for BAME attainment tend to suggest that the will to learn does not always translate into success. Perhaps this reemphasises the need for institutions to engage with their culturally diverse student groups.

Students need to learn to communicate with others across the different communities, irrespective of cultural background and native language. Educators need to shift the focus to meet these challenges, recognising that they must facilitate intercultural communication between students, bridge barriers to build resilience and develop the will to learn. Exploiting the transcultural flows within a diverse classroom, educators should support students in transitioning into higher education and support them in shaping new and possibly multicultural identities (Lam, 2006). Unfortunately, our own work, which chimes with other studies, has shown that these opportunities are only gained where there is true and meaningful interaction within the class and outside (Bamford & Pollard, 2018; Caruana, 2014; Gurin, Dey, Hurtado & Gurin, 2002). All too often, however, we found that students are hesitant to move across these culturally defined boundaries, preferring instead to stay in their familiar settings, 'self-segregating' in a sense (Bamford et al., 2015). Cross-cultural communication is important in the context of education and is deeply entrenched in the sense of belonging and academic success (Glass & Westmont, 2014). Degree programmes that promote discussion about race, religion and ethnicity have been shown to promote cross-cultural communication and engagement (Bamford et al., 2015; Gurin et al., 2002). These notions are explored in the subsequent chapters and provide a real insight into the importance of nurturing belonging across culturally diverse classrooms.

NOTES

1. The NSSE is an annual survey conducted in the United States and Canada that aims to assess the extent to which students engage in educational practices associated with high levels of learning and development.

2. Diverse perspectives are defined in E5 on Table 1.1.

3. The term 'commuter student' is one that is gaining some recognition in the literature. Pokorny, Holley, and Kane (2017) offer an example of this discussion.

CHAPTER 2

STRANGERS IN A NEW LAND

Αἴεν ἀριστεύειν καὶ ὑπείροχον ἔμμεναι ἄλλων

Ever to excel and be the best above all others.

The Iliad (Book 6, p. 208)

This quote from *The Iliad* forms part of a discussion between two characters about identity and having pride in the blood that you have inherited and bringing glory to your ancestors: it proposes that where you are from frames your activity and informs your actions. For us (the authors?), it carries the weight of the unchanging nature of human beings in understanding and knowing their connections, where they are from and where they are going to. The quote is the motto of several higher education institutions in this country and points to the achievements that universities expect and encourage in their students. Cultural identity and achievement are connecting factors that do not require the contemporary global shifts in politics and economics to be acknowledged but rather form part of our imaginings and aspirations and are thus inexorably akin to the higher education context.

Chapter 2 explores the narratives of first-generation migrants and the need for these students to appreciate cultural 'others' in the classroom so that all students feel included and have the capacity to develop the sense of belonging that some authors (Pokorny et al., 2017) recognise as important to the higher education learning experience.

In this chapter, we have drawn on the narratives of students who are first-generation migrants in order to better understand the feelings of distance, alienation and a sense of not belonging in the higher education setting. The intention here is not to explore the experience of those who come to this country specifically to study (i.e. those commonly referred to as International Students), but rather to give voice to the experiences of individuals who have migrated to the United Kingdom and then entered higher education at some point following their migration. The individuals' stories of their cultural journeys give 'voice' to those narratives and offer insights into their perceptions and lived experience. Our approach to culture here draws from the interpretive tradition of Clifford Geertz who tells us that:

> On the one level, there is a framework of beliefs, expressive symbols, and values in terms of which individuals define their world, express their feelings, and make their judgments; on the other level, there is the ongoing process of interactive behaviour, whose persistent form we call social structure. Culture is the fabric of meaning in terms of which human beings interpret their experience and guide their action; social structure is the form that action takes, the actually existing network of social relations. Culture and social structure are then but different abstractions from the same phenomena. The one considers social action in respect to its

> *meaning for those who carry it out, the other*
> *considers it in terms of its contribution to the*
> *functioning of some social system. (1973,*
> *pp. 144–145)*

This quote demonstrates that, for Geertz, the way individuals see and engage with the world is informed by their cultural perspectives, and social interactions are framed by their cultural meaning-making. These interpretations can vary across cultures and have the potential to cause disruption to those unfamiliar with others' meaning-making. The disruption may occur when situated engagement takes place where those with differing cultural scripts are required to interact with cultural others (Welikala & Watkins, 2008). It is the challenge of this difference that we witness being played out in the higher education environment where the social dimension of classroom interactions appears to play such an important role (Bamford & Pollard, 2018).

The students' experiences of the classroom are presented through the themes that emerged from their stories. We have considered the interrelation between the themes and their narratives in order to understand the experiences that first-generation migrant students face. The interviews evidenced obstacles, challenges and encounters that took place within a cultural frame and offered opportunities for learning that were both positive and negative. The narratives were based on students' interactions with both each other and their institutions. Recognising that the 'university experience' is more than just the 'classroom' (Gurin et al., 2002), the focus for our discussion is on students' cultural interactions both inside and outside the classroom. Gurin suggests that these broader interactions are fundamental to understand how the racial and ethnic diversity within universities impacts on students' learning experience. In this chapter, we discuss the experiences of individuals who had not participated in the UK education system prior to entering university. Their cultural experiences represent a transition not only in terms of the educational framework and their institution of study but also in terms of their belonging to the institution and the diverse student body that they now find themselves a member. Our research sought to understand the relevance of these interactions in terms of individuals' cultural journeys and transitions into their university studies and whether common themes could be found within their experiences. We recognised the importance of unpacking the transitions which are so often referenced in the literature but which remain not fully understood. For example, is the existential nature of such transitions in cultural terms tangible as part of the learning experience in higher education? There appears to be an acculturation (Berry & Ward, 2006) process that takes place when entering the university, but are there additional challenges and benefits that this unfamiliar and new higher education learning environment can bring to their experience?

Simply put, there are two potential levels of acculturation that need to be acknowledged as impactful transitions: firstly, living in the United Kingdom and, secondly, the university environment. Both of these offer (a — rather than 'two'?) new cultural frames of interaction. The students we interviewed are usually identified as 'home' students within university structures. Although there is some acknowledgement in recent literature around the experience of different groups of students and the potential for differing academic outcomes, this is rarely considered within a cultural frame. This chapter hopes to provide the reader with an understanding of students' different cultural backgrounds and the potential impact of these backgrounds at the level of the individual. In other words, a general categorisation of Black, Asian and Minority Ethnic (BAME) student does not differentiate students from a wide variety of different cultures, languages and backgrounds but instead uses the broad umbrella of BAME through which policy discussion is facilitated. Given the diversity of student bodies, our key question focuses around the link with the higher education experience and the exposure of students to cultural learning and whether higher education institutions acknowledge the impact and benefits. The cultural dissonance that we previously witnessed from differing groups both inside and outside the classroom (Bamford & Pollard, 2018) can be linked to Said's concepts of 'belonging and detachment, reception and resistance [...] insider and outsider' with regard to considering the processes involved in cultural interactions (Said, 2004, p. 76). Chapters 3, 4 and 5 consider in more detail the insider and outsider frameworks which are important in appreciating classroom interactions between students and which were raised by students both explicitly and implicitly.

For Said (2004), belonging and detachment are important considerations in cultural terms. Masika and Jones (2016) identify belonging themes such as being, doing, experiencing and becoming. These four aspects of the conceptual discussion around belonging might be viewed as fundamental elements of a true higher education experience and yet, as Gurin et al. (2002) recognise, the link between the curriculum in higher education and one's cultural identity and how that enables interaction with others remains the subject of much discussion. We have argued that (Bamford et al., 2015; Bamford & Pollard, 2018) cultural difference appears as an afterthought in academic terms for institutions, lecturers and students, but conversely appears central to the experience of higher education when the classroom experience is unpacked. It is certainly a truism that the impacts of cultural interactions are difficult to measure. They are reliant on subjective perspectives and variables such as personal engagement and resilience that are not easy to compare between one individual and another, and yet researchers continue to try to do so. Our research suggests that this is due to their defining impact on experience and thus education, reinforcing the importance of understanding Geertz' view of culture as being the fabric of meaning.

Perhaps the following quote from one of the interviewees, studying at a Russell Group institution in London, contextualises the conundrum we face as educators in exploring issues of reception and resistance, belonging and detachment and becoming. It reinforces the intangible nature and complexity of trying to understand cultural identity and its relationship with the education process and the impact of cultural interactions in diverse classrooms, and the essence of identity and relationships for the individuals involved.

> *[...] yeah, the cultural identity is as much of a conundrum as is consciousness. It really is and that's what I think (Parvinder, a Master's student from a Russell Group Institution in London)*

The interviews that were undertaken with first-generation migrants provide a narrative around these themes and each is considered through the lens of the individuals experiencing these dimensions of complexity. The tensions of insider and outsider, developing a sense of belonging and detachment from their cultural past and a sense of belonging to their cultural future, are of particular relevance. For many individuals, this might be presented through the development of resilience as a feature of acculturation.

The development of resilience, where resilience is defined by Liebenberg et al. as the 'the capacity of individuals to overcome adversity and do well in spite of exposure to significant adversity' (2012, p. 219), is a theme that was common amongst the first-generation migrants; their country of origin appeared to be less important. What is significant is the experience of adaption and dealing with the stress of the unfamiliar which is experienced on many levels. Bates and Miles-Johnson (2010, 2015b) identify resilience at three levels: individual attributes, family influences and cultural influences. In Bamford et al. (2015), we argued that students' resilience is linked not only to their engagement in the class-room, but also to their learning experience, and this resilience has a symbiotic relationship to their interaction with others. The data in that chapter thus supported the link with interactions with other students as being important. This premise supports Said's conviction (2004) with regard to the need to focus on humaneness, tolerance and recognition. Within the higher education environment, students' voices emphasise the need to understand the fundamental human qualities of those who are on cultural journeys in order to improve the learning experience.

2.1. CULTURAL JOURNEYS AND TRANSITIONS

2.1.1. Henry's Story

Henry is a first-generation migrant from Southern Africa, who came to the United Kingdom because of a relocation scheme offered by his employers in his home country. Clearly, a significant transition for him, and one that affected him strongly, was leaving his parental home and living by himself for the first time at the age of 19 in a neighbouring city. This was a steep learning curve for Henry: adapting to life as an adult, and looking after his own needs clearly had an impact even though he remained in close proximity to his parents. His migrant journey resulted from an opportunity that he seized due to a workplace restructure and the 'unbeatable offer' (to relocate to the United Kingdom). The move to another country did not initially present itself as so much of a challenge as the move from his parental home which was indeed impactful. Henry had a positive and all-embracing approach to life and he considered the move to the United Kingdom as simply another journey in his life, in keeping with others such as his training as a nurse and his business degree. His entry into higher education as a mature student was undertaken in order to seek a different direction to his career, especially in a new country. During the course of his undergraduate studies, he had become an informal mentor or even a father figure especially to some of the younger students whom he felt lacked direction and a clear understanding of why they were in university. He expressed concerns about the attitudes of younger students (who came from different second-generation backgrounds) to their learning and hoped to represent a receptive and belonging mode to those students rather than one of resistance and detachment. He believed that he had a responsibility to help his fellow students and felt it important to demonstrate an ethical position towards the guidance that he offered.

> *Coming back to the business management course, as we went through the prospectus, it sort of intrigued me that yes, this might be the right thing that I need in order to achieve where I want to be. Again, setting goals for myself and yeah — so I actually had to embark on this later, another journey. I registered with the [his university] for the business management course I'm actually doing at the moment. Still in my first year; yes, you meet different types of fellow students, it is a diverse environment if I can say, which does not present any*

*problem with me as well. I'm [...] sort of fit in very
well in any given situation. I adapt to situations,
let's put it that way, easily.*

*Now, the course in itself for me is, it means a lot, it's
like salvation because that is the password to getting
where I want to get. So this is why I am actually
showing commitment. I am very much aware of
what is required of the course. I try yes to do my
best and much as I jump around with my fellow
students, I actually am aiming for a first class and
I don't know about you guys but I'm aiming that
way. And they have sort of emulated and picked on
that and they are also aiming high as well because
I believe in challenges. I believe in competition,
rather I strive where there is competition, I like.
That is one of the things that actually gives me a
buzz and — look, the course I am not saying it's
smooth sailing. The journey is just like any other
journey, bumpy ride, but hey, you've got to pick
yourself up and brush yourself up and carry on.*

This excerpt demonstrates Henry's adaption and resilience and a strong sense of belonging to his institution.
Henry was very aware of the differing cultural scripts
(Welikala & Watkins, 2008) in the classroom and the ways
in which these behaviours can spill out into the corridors.
He worries also that his younger colleagues were too zealous in their haste to reject their own cultural identity as
they attempted to adopt to that of the university and that
this could have left them floundering. Henry's passion and
enthusiasm for his studies and helping his fellow students
may make his narrative appear repetitive but demonstrates
his desire to hone a point. He went further in recognising

the need for adaption but believes that younger generations can be too zealous in their approach.

> *Now they are trying to adapt new ways to reach –*
> *they're taking it way, way too far. Way, way too far*
> *than the actual sort of westernised people. It's like*
> *I try and adapt to your culture but then now, I get*
> *over zealous, that's why these youngsters are taking*
> *too big a bite and they can't chew it and they are all*
> *over the place.*

Henry felt that this tension manifests in a number of ways and he expressed concern about the impact of cultural dislodgment on the younger students. Drawing on his own experiences, he felt a need to guide them on their journey. Henry was proud of his heritage and whilst he recognised how comfortable he was in his host culture, he had not rejected or turned his back on his own culture, appreciating how his cultural journey to date had informed him as an individual. It is important to observe how Henry's perception of cultural dissonance, which he believed to be an effect of students trying to 'fit it' and 'adapt', was so keenly expressed. For universities, it could be seen as an opportunity for them to foster a more inclusive and supportive environment for the culturally diverse student body.

2.1.2. Bode's Story

Bode, who was born in Nigeria, came to live in this country as a young adult following an initial emigration to London and then to Ireland with his parents. He went to school in Dublin and spent most of his formative years in Ireland. His story is one of determination and resilience, despite the cultural differences that he experienced, including a substantial

amount of racial abuse. Recognising that whilst there are
similarities between the English and Irish education systems,
there remain cultural differences that are inherent and documented between the two countries and we are therefore confident that Bode's secondary education in Ireland represents
sufficient difference to make his migration to the United
Kingdom as a young adult relevant to this chapter. The
excerpt below offers an insight into his resilience and
adjustment.

> I used to live in England when I was younger but
> then I moved to Dublin. So I came from Nigeria
> when I was a lot younger, moved to London, stayed
> for about two years then moved to Dublin around
> 2006, around that time. So I grew up most of my
> time in Dublin. And when I went to Dublin at first,
> I was the only black guy in my school, it was crazy,
> I was like, wow, this is hard. Unlike when I was
> here in school and it was just me and I was – it was
> quite intimidating at first. But then there's always –
> there was a problem back then because I was still on
> my own so there was the racial problems still. But
> then, I cannot twist that the whole racial problem,
> I kind of made it into a positive way for me because
> as I told you, I am the only black guy in the school.
> So that means if I do anything it's gonna be unique
> because I'm the only – so it's just gonna be me.
>
> So I started playing rugby for the secondary school
> because I was quite fast and I was quite strong, the
> team loved me, then from the [...]the whole school
> started knowing about me and they got to love me
> and I wasn't that black guy any more. I was oh
> Bode is on the rugby team, then [...] so that kind of

*helped me, growing up in Dublin kind of helped me
deal with the racial abuse and the racial issues
because it just made me grow up quicker because
I was the only black guy there. So it just made me
grow up more.*

*It wasn't, there was nothing physical, it was just
more the verbal use. Like 'go back to your country,
you monkey, go back' – There was one time I was
playing at rugby actually against a different
secondary school, [...] The person who was meant
to mark me, and he was just making some racial
abuse 'now go back, you monkey go back to the
jungle' things like that. But then I didn't take, it was
like you know what, I'm that type of person that it
really takes a lot for you to get me angry. Maybe
because of the way I was raised up, I don't get
angry easily, I just overlook things most of the time
and I just let it go by.*

*So yeah, I got most of the verbal abuse 'oh you
monkey, go back to –' the 'n' word and all of that.
So that was the extreme but people just speaking
out. But I'm not getting any physical abuse or
anything like that, it's just the verbal. But then if [...]
as I said, it just depends on who you are as a
person. I just always blocked every word they said
and I didn't allow it to get to me so I think that was
the good way of dealing with such issues, just not
allowing them to get to you.*

On the whole, Bode remained positive and embarked on a
new degree in London. He demonstrated a strong insider perspective with regard to his current higher education institution and the desire to encourage belonging in other students.

This is evidenced by formalising his belonging in a sabbatical position with the Students Union. His resilience, expressed through his ability to overcome the abuse he was subjected to as a child and his determination to succeed, has been informed by his experiences. He was a young man who was focused on setting goals for his achievements, again recognising that he was on a journey that would present challenges both positive and negative but that would result in him reaching his achievements. This chimes with Henry's journey and offers other students an insight into how success is made possible through the learning and resilience which developed as challenges were met and overcome.

2.1.3. Marie's Story

Marie had a very different outlook to her journey to Bode and Henry, although she did paint a similar picture of resilience and determination to succeed. Her views were more negatively expressed because of the struggle that she felt she had undertaken. She too was keen to talk so that others would benefit and could draw from her experiences of challenge and success. Her concern was that others could struggle but she wanted them to understand that it is possible to succeed. Marie came to the United Kingdom as a migrant from the Ivory Coast and her children were all born in the United Kingdom. She migrated more than 10 years before going to university; she was a native French speaker and felt she had struggled with learning English. Despite having finished her degree in law with Lower Second Class honours and moving on to Law School in the United Kingdom, she continued to struggle with English as a non-native speaker. Her degree was her second attempt at undergraduate study having attempted a different undergraduate course in the North of

England. Her English language ability appeared to be closely linked with her sense of belonging although there was a strong sense of identity and belonging displayed to the United Kingdom. Her desire to speak out was in part driven by a desire to help universities understand the struggles of those who were non-native speakers of English; the struggles of those who had tragedy visited upon them during their studies as well as the impact of having no one to talk it through with. Her tragedy and isolation dominated her narrative. Maria had lost her partner during her final year of studies and whilst she understood the pressures of final-year study in a subject such as Law, she felt she had not been 'heard' in a personal sense as she could not attend university after her partner passed away. Her struggle evidenced outsider per-spectives and this was strongly linked to language and the importance of being supported in the university environment to achieve her goals. Throughout her narrative, she made ref-erence to feeling distanced and the 'family' identity that she craved as a student of a university which she felt simply never materialised. The challenges to her confidence and language ability are evidenced in the excerpt below:

> *Yes, it's a problem because first of all when I was studying so I would translate my French into English, and that wasn't helping because it was difficult for me and sometimes my lecturer would correct my work and say it doesn't make sense, it doesn't make sense, you get rejected. So at the end I said ok, let me study English and just if anything is bad or not just write it and that's how I started writing. But then I couldn't finish because we had a political war in my country so that affected me, I couldn't finish and I couldn't finish [...] I finished with a diploma in higher education.*

*Yes, so I couldn't finish. So I stopped and [...]
because my background was not wealthy, we moved
to London from Stockton, we moved here. And then
because I was finding my own business and then
because we came here the business went down and
I couldn't get a job afterwards. So I was planning to
go back to study and I said ok I am going to do [...]
And then my friend said you know since you were
[...] training, because back home I was training to
become a judge. And she said that was your dream
to become a judge and you want to be a solicitor
here, why don't you go for it? And I'm like no, my
English is not good, I can't do it and she's like your
English is perfect, go for it. I said they will not take
me; my English is no good. She said 'try' and then
I tried and I got this offer*

Marie talks of her sense of disappointment with the university systems that she encountered and the sense of abandonment that she felt as a result.

*[...] You have to − I was studying in [former
university name] and I was with [...][...], most of
them were English. And there was no like ok, you
have to come here to work on your writing because
this is not your first language. So there is nothing,
you just − if you are here then you have to be ready
to follow [...] here in [current university name], it's
quite diverse and that's what is worrying me about
ok, they're doing well, they open the door to
students to come here but they have also to put
something in place to help those students. I don't
know about it, maybe some of them might achieve
what their target is but I think it's difficult.*

There are clear signs of insider mentality with regard to her institution demonstrated here, in other words a sense of belonging. However, she strongly expresses the importance of university support and this notion of 'struggling' alone as she sees it.

> This university will follow me all my life because I was here, So if tomorrow I find out that the university [...] they are talking about it in a good way, that would also reflect on me [...] If there is something I need to raise then I will so that they can improve [...]

Belonging and attachment are expressed again here as key aspects of this narrative as well as a pride and engagement with her institution, witnessed through Marie's repeated insistence that universities must provide the support that enables students to achieve their goals. Marie felt that it was incumbent upon universities to recognise the potential weaknesses that students bring with them. Marie also expressed concern that there were additional challenges attached to being a commuter student in London, stating that there is not enough time to devote to study because the urban environment is steeped in everyone 'rushing' to their destinations.

2.1.4. Parvinder's Story

Parvinder was an Anthropology student in her early 20s and was studying at a Russell Group institution. She considered that her identity was international and she did not identify with one particular culture because her family had moved around since she was young. Her parents were from Pakistan originally but she grew up in Canada and then moved to the Middle East. Her family, who she described as comfortably off, continued to live in the Middle East although she had close family in the United Kingdom. She was raised in an international environment with others who were the children of diplomats and had many cultural experiences as a result. Despite this, she felt the main cultural transitions that she had gone through were in London; on reflecting on the reasons for this, it was difficult for her to pin down whether this was due to her age, level of independence or the environment in London. She clearly felt that the people she had met in London had shaped her outlook and approach to life, particularly in the music scene. Her parents were not traditional although they had tried to embed a sense of cultural identity in their children and maintained cultural traditions but she felt that in London she had broken away from her traditional background.

She found that the London music scene offered a cultural fluidity that she had not experienced elsewhere. Parvinder enthused that it offered the ability to connect culturally with others and develop a stronger sense of belonging than she had felt before. She attributed this to a common connection to the music which achieved a cosmopolitan environment for communication. The breaking down of barriers was key to cultural integration, and music was the vehicle that had helped her to do this. Her feeling of freedom to think and act was expressed in terms of cultural growth in London. She acknowledged that a challenge for her had been presented by being questioned by contemporaries about her former lifestyle in the Middle East, and she accepted that she needed to correct misconceptions, such as the fact that she had not gone to school on a camel. She was measured in her discussion of this misconception but affirmed that it was a presumption that was often made. One of her biggest transitions was in understanding the difference between US education, where she had received her formative education, and that of the UK education system. She had struggled to understand that as part of a Russell Group institution in London, she would not have the closed campus experience most US institutions offer by providing a strong university identity and facilitating a sense of belonging and of family. For her, this perhaps might be viewed in tribal terms such as supporting the college football team. This again alludes to the pervasive aspect of London institutions where engagement issues are challenged by a dispersion of the student body and the impact of 'commuting'. This may reinforce the notion of cultural identity provided by the music scene which Parvinder embraced and enabled her to feel a 'Londoner'.

2.1.5. Abdul's Story

Abdul was born in Syria and had been living in London for 10 years. He grew up in Morocco where he undertook his university education in French despite being a native Arabic speaker. Following his university education, he worked for a Japanese motor company as an auditor but decided to pursue doctoral study in the United Kingdom because of the reputation of British higher education, even though he had questions about the nature of British culture; assumptions that English people were cold and/or football hooligans were cited as examples. These questions and their stereotypical assumptions influenced his perspectives and caused him to carefully consider his choice of coming to the United Kingdom. However, when he moved to the United Kingdom, these suppositions were quickly challenged and he enjoyed living in the country.

> So yes, my perception changed of the world, it
> changed of myself as well. I think the French system

*was very orthodox, disciplined, strict, you don't
say certain things, you don't do certain other
things. In England, you do whatever you want as
long as you are within the limits of the law or with
what you call the ethic or the morals, you will be
fine. So I liked this freedom: I would say, I loved it.
I'd like to think that I thrived a bit on this because
after my Masters I got a scholarship to do a PhD
[...] I think he (my supervisor) was trusting me
enough to say I'd like you to apply for a PhD
scholarship, I think you've got what it takes to be a
top researcher. Maybe because he said it but at that
time I thought No he's just trying to be nice, he's
being English again.*

*I started the PhD, it was really hard, the hardest bit
in terms of my studies in the UK was the PhD, the
first six months of the PhD. It killed me because you
needed to come with something novel and for me –
for the duration of my studies, for whatever time
I spent at university I was always given the
information I was asked to develop it, criticise it,
analyse it, report back, do a presentation. It was
mainly the descriptive part with [...] or in the PhD
I was asked to come up with something new. Plus
the pressure of being a PhD scholar which means
you need to finish within 3 years otherwise they kick
you out.*

This excerpt underlines not just the impact of cultural difference but movement and adaption, awareness and understanding as well as what could be perceived as continued stereotypical assumptions that underpin the cultural context of higher education.

One of the striking elements of Abdul's story is the sense of liberation that he feels his UK university education has given him, as well as living in the United Kingdom. Abdul also appreciated the support that he received from a number of staff, and mentioned their names several times, making it clear that these individuals were pivotal in his journey.

> *I love this country [...]. Because it gave me everything I have now and I'm loving everything about what I am doing right now. It was a dream, 10, 15, 20 years ago to be sat in the middle of [name of] Park in a beautiful university, in a beautiful city, surrounded by people from everywhere. The variety of knowledge, the variety of backgrounds, being able to improve every single day, being able to seek help or ask.*

Like Henry, Abdul was very aware of the cultural differences being played out in the classroom and the need to be sensitive to these differences; he echoed Henry's views that it is important to be proud of the heritage that he brought with him.

2.2. CULTURAL JOURNEYS AND OBSTACLES

A strong theme that emerged from our interviews was that these first-generation migrants, whilst they had acculturated to their new environment in the United Kingdom, had a strong sense of their cultural identity, who they were and where they were from. This presented to us a different picture to those who were second- and third-generation migrants, as discussed in Chapter 3, and this appeared significant to us. There seemed to be no disruption to their cultural sense-making or even a disruption to their sense of cultural identity. This does not seem to be the case with those students who come from second- and third-generation migrants' back-grounds which we explore more fully in Chapter 3. It is worth noting at this stage that social capital may also play a significant part in such students' ease of transition (Cross & Atinde, 2015) and again this will be explored further in Chapter 3. The transition of the students discussed in this chapter appeared smoother from their perspective than for students in the later chapters, and their narratives demonstrated their resilience and determination to succeed in the UK university environment. This smoother transition that was evidenced may reflect their confidence in their own cultural identity. Transition is determined by a complex mix of factors, but is sometimes linked to age, level of education and the perceived economic advantages when assimilation is achieved. An overriding factor evidenced in their narratives can be seen as the 'will to learn' (Barnett, 2007) which drives their engagement. Additionally, the adage that travel broadens the mind appears pertinent here — there is evidence that age and cultural capital are relevant to the ability to make further transitions such as the one to university. Both Henry and Bode were very proud of their cultural identity and used this as capital in their interaction with others.

The narratives also indicated a sense of personal struggle on their journeys into UK higher education and these individuals were able to draw on those experiences such as adaption and transition as they continued with their studies. Parvinder's story appeared different as she had a more cosmopolitan ethos and that, whilst she was a migrant, her arrival in the United Kingdom was more recent than some of the others, and she lived in a continual state international mobility. Her resulting cosmopolitan outlook that was threaded throughout her narrative helped her to transition to new surroundings easily and facilitated a cultural fluidity that others did not express. However, her narrative also hints at an inner resilience as a consequence of childhood international mobility and a number of significant international transitions that she felt made her 'international' as opposed to identifying a particular national identity. Luthar (2006) defines resilience as a phenomenon or process reflecting relatively positive adaptation despite the experiences of significant adversity or trauma. Migration can be seen in a context of resilience when individuals are forced to deal with new and unfamiliar cultural environments. It frames our understanding of a cultural journey and brings it into sharp focus. Reich, Zautra, and Hall (2010) suggest that resilience can be regarded as an element of human capital, providing migrants with the ability to navigate successfully through their new environment in their 'quest for a goal'.

The drivers who have resulted in the migration by individuals are evidenced in the move into the university environment as part of their 'quest'. The relevance of the degree to their desired outcomes also seems to support the building of resilience, particularly for the mature students who have chosen university in order to change the direction of their lives and reap economic benefits from the outcome. Whilst we could write at length on the issues of human capital and resilience, the focus for this current work only permits us to acknowledge the potential effects and the importance of such push-pull factors.

As Chiswick and DebBurman (2004) point out, first-generation migrants often find it difficult to convert their previous educational experiences into equal employment opportunities when they enter a new country and are therefore more invested in their educational experience when they move to a new country. This resonates strongly with Marie's story and, in part, may explain why she persisted in her studies, in spite of the barriers that she experienced. Marie clearly felt that her institution did not support her in achieving her

goals and, on several occasions, expressed her disappointment with the level of support. The underlying theme to this
is the need to develop a sense of belonging and family. Henry
became a father figure and Bode a mentor. Henry clearly felt
that his maturity and experience could help his fellow students, and whilst Bode did not articulate this as clearly, his
decision to be a sabbatical officer evidenced this. Not only
did Henry and Bode feel that they belonged but also they
knew that they could help others in their academic journey.
Family appeared key to these students: Abdul was offered a
father figure by the institution; Parvinder created a family
with the London music scene; and Marie was still looking for
hers but evidenced a strong sense and a desire for intervention to help others.

This theme of 'family' counters a view that cultural migration creates an element of resistance as the cultural resistance
identified by Said (2004) did not appear as a theme in the
interviews with regard to students' experience in university.
Perhaps the resistance occurred earlier, prior to entry to university as part of their cultural journey which developed both
in terms of their resilience and in terms of their ability to
belong. The language of 'outsider' did not feature in their
university cultural interactions but *becoming and belonging*
was evident through their narratives of their cultural journey.

These interviews provide a valuable insight into how first-
generation migrants relate to others in the classroom. Not
one of them expressed a sense of poor fit but, on the con-
trary, was able to reflect a positive contribution. These are
students who belong in the classroom and want to create a
sense of community and family. These are students who have
already adapted to cultural change; they are used to new
environments; when faced with challenges in university, they
are not phased, but find positive outcomes.

CHAPTER 3

'LEAVING CULTURE AT THE CLASSROOM DOOR'

The focus for this book is to better understand the students' cultural journeys, and, in this chapter, we turn our attention to the experiences of second- and third-generation migrants. The challenges with seemingly 'feeling university' (a term used by Lehmann, 2007, to evoke the sense of not fitting in to the university habitus) are threaded throughout the narratives presented in this chapter. The narratives allowed us to delve into the ways in which the traditionally Anglo-Saxon higher education environment in England is perceived by these culturally diverse students in terms of their transition and participation. Benhabib (2002) highlights the importance of understanding cultural difference in contemporary society in his work on culture in the global era. In our view, the higher education classroom offers an opportunity to witness the potential for cultural understanding and relationality to develop. However, the literature and our data evidence that we need to 'distil coherence out of the multiplicity of conflicting narratives and practices' so that educators can be 'attentive to the positioning and repositioning of the other and the self, of 'us' and 'them' in this complex dialogue' and that is brought into sharp focus in cultural diverse classrooms (Benhabib, 2002, p. 41). The cultural encounters that are inevitably part of our students' journeys form an aspect of the educational experience that has been given insufficient attention.

The students whose stories are recounted in this chapter can be distinguished from international students and first-generation migrants because the latter have experienced primary and secondary education in the United Kingdom, identified themselves as British despite coming from different ethnic backgrounds[1] and have already negotiated between the cultural worlds of home and school life. Our previous work has shown that the cultural dynamics that students from different cultural backgrounds bring to the classroom are often unnoticed by their institutions (Bamford et al., 2015) and yet we find here that their journeys to and throughout university do not always mirror those of either home or international students in terms of the focus given to those groups. Thus, they appear to us to be a neglected group as they do not fall within a traditional home student definition; they may not speak English at home (Bamford et al., 2015); and yet they are not considered to be culturally different enough to be identified as international. Our research led us to question whether their values and belief systems chime with traditional Anglo-Saxon norms of behaviour in the higher education setting. This chapter focuses on culturally fitting in. The issue of the potential dissonance that arises is explored further in Chapter 4.

It is not unusual for the students who tell their story in this chapter to be the first of their families to enter UK higher education. For many of them, university offers a doorway into a world that is unfamiliar and not always easy to navigate as they do not have the cultural capital that others from more traditional backgrounds may have. Their stories highlight their preconceptions, misunderstandings and personal journeys, as transitions are made into university life. The narratives of students from five different institutions are retold here and echo some of the key foci of the previous chapter.

In order to contextualise the stories, we pick up on this thread of 'feeling university' and developing a sense of belonging, as linking factors recognised in contributing to student persistence and motivation (Hausmann, Schofield, & Woods, 2007; Tinto, 1987). Most of the literature on belonging puts Tinto's model of student departure (1987) at its centre. Tinto purports that students who fail to persist at university do so because they are unable to integrate both socially and academically, both of which are fundamental to assimilation, acceptance and fitting in. The model recognises that students bring with them their own attributes, experiences and levels of preparedness, which are the aspects that we too recognise from the insights that these interviews offered. Tinto's work has gained considerable support in the literature (in the literature?) and perhaps the suggestion of the importance of integration as part of the educational experience is easy to identify with; however, there is little empirical evidence to support this model of persistence.

The key to persistence appears to be strongly linked with knowing what are the cultural rules and norms of behaviour which, in turn, mean that you can belong. The structural basis for higher education in England is indubitably modelled on a traditional Anglo-Saxon model which can appear intangible in its norms and rules to some. What is evident is that persistence is needed to navigate the cultural barrier that is presented to those coming from the non-traditional backgrounds, as are discussed in this chapter.

Vaccaro, Newman, and Daly-Cano (2015) suggest persistence may be of particular importance to those students who sit outside the 'traditional' student body and sit on the margins. Thayer (2000) argues that these non-traditional students (i.e. students from lower socio-economic groups who are often first-generation university students) are disadvantaged and suggests that there are different dimensions to this sense of disadvantage. Whilst there is often a belief that such students are disadvantaged because they lack the social and cultural capital that supports success, an interesting counterview is offered by Cross and Atinde (2015). They argue that 'disadvantaged' students should not be condemned to failure as they are able to develop educational assets through the academic challenges they encounter, again building on concepts of persistence (Cross & Atinde, 2015). Thayer (2000) wonders if they sit on the margins of the different cultures that they represent – their past culture (the one they left at home) and their current culture (the culture of the university).

Tinto's argument on the need for student persistence emphasises that student belonging, self-efficacy and the valuing of the curriculum are motivators for learning (Tinto, 1987). These factors, whilst linked, play out differently for each individual student, depending on the advantage, and disadvantage, witnessed as a subjective aspect of each cultural journey. Tinto describes the engagement and sense of belonging that occurs when students feel that they are a part of the community and that they are valued for their participation by their academic institution. Tinto distinguishes between simply forming a bond with a small group of students and bonding with the larger institution itself. This multi-layered engagement is discussed in more detail in the next chapter. It is the latter that is the more important in terms of student belonging and participation, but how easily this occurs depends largely on students' past experiences, and the perception students have of how they are viewed by those around them. Naturally this is altered by the diverse mix of staff and students within the classroom and the university itself; students who do not have peers or academics to whom they can relate are more likely to feel out of place (Gale & Parker, 2014).

According to Thayer (2000), first-generation students are less likely to have someone in their life with first-hand experience of university, and limited knowledge of university systems and the bureaucracy that universities often wrap themselves in. The importance of cultural capital in terms of Said's categories of adjustment and adaption is seen to be played out time and time again in the narratives (and has been explored in our previous chapter).

This is a view articulated by Thomas who states:

> *educational institutions are able to determine what values, language and knowledge are regarded as legitimate, and therefore ascribe success and award qualifications on this basis. Consequently, pedagogy is not an instrument of teaching, so much as of socialization and reinforcing status [...] individuals who are inculcated in the dominant culture are the most likely to succeed, while other students are penalized. (Thomas, 2002, p. 431)*

The narratives that are presented in this chapter underline the complexities of individuals' socialisation into university life. What we can see in Farah's story below is a journey full of ups and downs, with issues that centre around her family life that evidence her struggles, her adjustment and her unfamiliarity with higher education that impact on her adaption and persistence.

3.1. FARAH'S STORY

Farah came to the institution in which we met her after drop-
ping out from another university which she had joined directly after completing a BTEC course in college. Her journey
illustrates her struggles and fortitude. She is the youngest of
four children to parents who immigrated to the United
Kingdom from Bangladesh. Neither her parents nor her siblings had a strong educational background, and whilst her
brother started at university, he did not complete his studies.
She summarised the educational experience of her parents in
the following way:

> *My parents — I actually asked them a few weeks
> ago in fact, so in your childhood did you go for any
> sort of training, further development? And they said
> no simply because of the strain of having such a
> young family and bringing them up. So, they didn't
> feel that they actually had the time to do further
> development. So, I myself never actually really saw
> my parents pick up books.*

The last sentence above portrays the distance that needs
to be travelled for some students and the potential importance and influence of socio-economic background. In
Farah's case, this can be seen in terms of highlighting the difference that she felt between where she came from and where
she was going to. In the literature, this is often referred to as
the transition (Thomas, 2002) to a university environment,
which can vary in terms of impact from individual to individual but was evident for nearly all the students when discussing their cultural journeys. Secondary education gave
Farah a sense of freedom that she had not previously experienced and it led her to become slightly rebellious and to take
risks.

> *So back then, I was happy as Larry, went to school,*
> *got to 14/15, that's when I moved to, that's when*
> *I found myself a personality which wasn't the*
> *brightest [...] But I travelled on the bus and I had a*
> *little bit more freedom which I never really thought*
> *but when I had it, it was like oh, ok, I can do things*
> *against the law. Not that it was an interest back*
> *then, it was just that it's something that [...] So [...]*
> *crowds and I got [...] a bit of trouble.*

A moment of self-realisation led her to seek support and discipline from her teachers, which ensured that she studied and successfully completed her GCSEs. Farah moved from school to college to study for her BTEC diploma. She talks again of freedom and that the freedom she experienced enabled her to try new things. Her story suggests a layering of transition points, of building confidence through each of her educational experiences:

> *I went to a local college and eventually became the*
> *ambassador of that college. College for me was the*
> *best time of my life because I was so on top of*
> *everything I was doing. I was able to focus on the*
> *gym, that I'm a trainer, I enjoyed singing so I would*
> *end up going to the studio. I had time for*
> *everything, I had time for my family, I had time to*
> *work, I had time for college, I had time to be with*
> *all of my friends.*

She expressed surprise that her family allowed her to move away from home when she progressed to university. Despite being a bright and capable student, Farah found she was left to struggle, juggling a disability that she had and the transition to university. She had not made reference to her disability until this point which perhaps reflects that, in this new environment, it became an issue for her. At her former institution, she found it difficult to obtain information about the support that should have been available and she often expresses a sense of being 'othered' by the process.

> *I didn't feel part of the university; I didn't know that there was disability support up until I applied to come to university this year. So, I went to university when I was 20, I left at 23 so I repeated my first year, not knowing I could actually have mitigating circumstances.*

Farah left her first university after her second year, having been largely ignored by the support systems. Her experience was negative and the distance she felt from her educational institution is evidenced throughout her narrative. The struggles and challenges she endured were notable elements of her experience.

Farah was all too aware of the sacrifices that her parents have made and makes frequent reference to their struggle as opposed to her own struggle with a long-term medical condition.

> *It was a different type of struggle but I never knew [...] struggle until [...] My parents struggled through — they got there in the end but why should life be so hard, why are we in this world or in this country to struggle and struggle and struggle just to make ends meet? Where do you enjoy living? Where do you enjoy your children, where do you enjoy your partner, where do you enjoy going alone at the end of the day?*

This is a story of great personal challenges, resilience and perseverance which is markedly different from Ben's story below. Farah graduated with an Upper Second Class honours degree, having joined the degree from a different institution. In the end, she felt her new institution offered her the support she needed and she felt able to belong. This sense of belonging was important to her, both in terms of not feeling the alienation she had previously felt and in terms of her building resilience and coping with her struggles. Her sense of personalisation of her educational experience was evident in her narrative and clearly an important factor in her transition to her new institution.

3.2. BEN'S STORY

Ben was a Master's student at a London Russell Group university. He was brought up by his mother and his maternal grandmother. He talks of his grandmother's Irish background, but does not feel her background impacted on him in any measurable way in spite of the fact that his father was also from an Irish background. When pushed, Ben describes himself as English, but articulates a strong intercultural understanding, and a fascination in cultures unfamiliar to him. This is exemplified by his linguistic ability. Ben began teaching himself Ancient Greek at the age of 12, and his interest in the language led him to continue with this area of study at university. His narrative conveys a strong sense of determination that differentiates him from some of the other students and their narratives.

> *And that's where it all started basically so I did reasonably well with that and I thought well, ever wanting to overstep and to excel and to do the best that I can, I tried to get on to other ones and absorb as much as I can. So that you asked where was the beginning, it's as simple as that, going with that flow.*

This excerpt illustrates traits of adaption, determination and a will to succeed. Whilst, on the face of it, the sense of determination and confidence portrays a difference to Farah's journey, the strong elements of adaption witnessed in his narrative are mirrored in other narratives to varying degrees and we believe this leads to the development of belonging.

Ben's educational journey led him to a small specialist college. Perhaps because much of his knowledge was self-learnt (as he was privately tutored), Ben sees education as not being confined to institutions but gained through experiences, although he is quick to acknowledge the academic uniqueness that universities bring. This experiential dimension to culture in the sense that it is experienced from the reality of each individual is acknowledged by Benhabib (2002) and it is from individuals' cultural realities that we can construct the narrative needed to understand their educational journeys and address the claims made in the name of culture. The higher education journeys of these students chime with Benhabib's understanding of cultures as complex human practices of signification and representation, of organisation and attribution, which are internally driven by conflicting narratives. This experience, attribution and internally driven narrative are evidenced in the excerpt below from Ben:

> *David Beckham, for all his virtues, did not receive a university education at Manchester United, even though he says my footballing education was at Manchester United, whatever. So yes, interaction with foreign cultures can be a type of education, of course, if we use the word* lato sensu *in the broad sense. But in a strictly narrow sense, which is the goal of university, I don't think it is because the goal of university is academic education, which is something more strict in its meaning.*

This is an interesting perspective and does not echo some of the other narratives, in terms of the confidence and self-assurance that is displayed from this interviewee.

Although the university Ben attended boasted a strong multicultural experience, Ben was aware of the whiteness of university culture. Interestingly, he praised his institution for being 'uniquely multicultural'.

> *The word multicultural is bandied around a lot in modern Britain but I think that [the institution] is actually a genuine example of multiculturalism where you have the entire gamut of all the world's cultures [...] interacting equally. And you have cultural information and you have a cultural sharing. Multiculturalism in Britain, it doesn't seem to work on a societal level as well as it does at [the institution] for instance.*

Whilst Ben notes the multicultural dimensions of the institution where he studied, he suggests that it is the responsibility of the student to adapt:

> *I've never seen it myself personally but I am fairly sure that a young 18-year-old girl who's never been outside her village in China and gets a scholarship to come and study at [the university] will perhaps find herself a bit culturally disconnected. I'm sure you would have to be ignorant to deny that happens. But I think that's, perhaps, that's part of the process of becoming more secure in one's self [...] I don't think cultural integration is a target, is a goal of the university, [...] university?*

This underlines Ben's confidence in his abilities as well of those of others at university. Although the evidence of this confidence may appear to separate him from others, it is also seen in the narrative of Parvinder in Chapter 2, who studied at the same Russell Group institution. This confidence could be seen as a reflection of the both students' socio-economic background and cosmopolitanism (Bamford & Pollard, 2018).

Ben clearly integrated into his university and had a strong sense of belonging. He depicts his home culture as 'a very traditional conservative household', describing it as 'British culture itself' and this may be why he found it so easy to transition into the very traditional world that his institution embodied. As he eloquently puts it:

> [...] the fact of the matter is, academic education in so many subjects, physics, chemistry, all the sciences, biology, is western, all of it was invented by quote, unquote, white people up until the middle of the 20th century.

His interest in language gave him an appreciation of cultures and his own experiences led him to look at similarities not differences.

> I do believe that fundamentally the human experience is something that is very uniform in its most basic elements actually [...] If I'm going to feel uncomfortable I'm going to feel uncomfortable in modern British culture as much as Taiwanese culture, that's my view. I would say that with regards to cultural identification, I'd say a lot of it as well is a process of individuation whereby the person tries to separate themselves from their peers, consciously, voluntarily alienating themselves in order to stand out. I would say that is a factor as well. And that's controversial but I think that's true. So, for instance, me, if I start going on about how

> *I'm Irish or I'm Irish descent and how wonderful*
> *that is, and then I think to myself that I'm being*
> *alienated from society because I'm Irish [...] I'm not*
> *being alienated from the society because I'm Irish,*
> *that's a process of voluntary, self-alienation in order*
> *to individuate myself and in order to give myself*
> *some kind of identity, that's what I think.*

Belonging is a key part of Ben's journey. He conveyed a strong sense of fit and understanding of the higher education culture that he found himself in but indicated that culture has no place in the classroom. This is confirmed in Surinder's narrative below which is from a slightly different perspective but with a view which confirms the notion of separation of individuals' cultural identity and the classroom environment.

Interestingly, whilst Ben appreciates the multicultural dimensions of his institution, his narrative suggests that the university should not be proactive in addressing the culturally diverse classroom dynamic. Instead, he appears to believe that all too often students self-alienate or don't adapt, and he suggests that they should do more to fit in. It is worth noting that Ben came to higher education from a family of academics and has the cultural and, perhaps, social capital which enabled an ease of being that was common in very few of the interviewees – perhaps with the exception of Parvinder (see Chapter 2). The possibility of differences in cultural journeys for these two individuals may reside in confidence and ease of cultural adaption due to a more cosmopolitan perspective with which they come to university.

3.3. SURINDER'S STORY

Surinder's educational journey was perhaps more traditional, in the sense that she moved from a UK primary school to a private secondary school and then moved directly to her university. Surinder conveys a sense that going to university was a natural progression for her. She was born in the United Kingdom but both of her parents were originally from Sri Lanka. After completing her secondary education in a mixed grammar school just outside Watford, Surinder was accepted to study Law and Criminology at a university in the North of England and was in her final year when she was interviewed. Surinder clearly enjoyed the cultural diversity that her university offered and also the town in which it is located.

> *I honestly am so glad now I've ended up there because it is really diverse and I've met so many different people there. And I just genuinely just love the city.*

The very positive transition to her new environment is indicated in this statement. However, this strong connection and easy transition may directly relate to a confidence instilled in her by her private education. Whilst Surinder talks about the strong sense of diversity at university and cites this as a key reason for choosing her university, she is also aware of the lack of integration amongst her peers.

> *There is definitely a segregation in that way when you go to Uni because you have the people who are international who are Sri Lankan and Tamil or Indian or whatever. And as British people we tend to just stick with British people and they tend to do their own thing. We all know — and it's not like there's a competition or anything like that, but there is definitely a difference and everybody knows [...] Yes, it's sort of like that's what I know is that all my friends have been of my similar kind of background or similar skin colour so I thought that's my*

> *comfort, it is a kind of comfort. And it's like if I'm*
> *gonna — it's my first day, if I'm gonna know that*
> *I can somehow make a connection with anybody it's*
> *gonna be someone like that. I remember going up*
> *and thinking I need to make friends now; this is the*
> *only time. And my instinct was to go to someone*
> *who was Asian, and she ended up being one of my*
> *friends. So, it's just an instinct so I don't really know*
> *where that comes from.*

Although pushed on this matter a little more, Surinder was unable to articulate a reason for this sense of bonding with culturally similar students, other than it was a comfortable place for her, a sense of fit perhaps that enables her to belong. The safe space of culturally familiar norms and frameworks appeared to be a strong pull factor both with regard to her choice of institution and with regard to her social circles at university. The push factor was the need for independence from her family and whilst this was not overtly discussed in other narratives, many journeys describe the potency of breaking away from home cultures. With time, Surinder began to embrace other cultures on campus and to build relationships with other students.

> *When I came to [the university] I just met so many*
> *different kinds of people and where they were from*
> *and not even just people from my culture, people*
> *who are from Sri Lanka, like international students*
> *from Malaysia who are Tamils. And just so many*
> *different types of people and they'd done [...] things*
> *they were exposed to like, they were so different to*
> *us in a way like the way they did things, the way*
> *they dressed and stuff.*

Surinder felt strongly that the university she was attending could do more to bring cultures together and felt that she was able to fit in better because of her English accent.

Yeah, I think being British has helped me and obviously for the English from day one here, they've helped me I think. And as soon as I start speaking to people they just know that I'm from [...].

She spoke of the university's international centre and international activities as somewhat divisive.

But in terms of integrating they should definitely try and be more like, this is not just for international events. Even [...] anybody else is free to come along, it's sort of like − but not really.

Surinder exuded academic confidence and also described a clear sense of belonging at university, which stems in part from her ability to cross the different cultures that she represents. Like Ben, she too was enjoying the diversity of her university but, interestingly, sought out those who are culturally similar to her. In contrast to Ben, however, she felt that her institution should do more to support the culturally diverse nature of the classroom.

3.4. ALISHA'S STORY

Alisha was born in the United Kingdom to Pakistani parents and knew from an early age that she wanted to become a primary school teacher, but never believed this would become a reality because her parents had a different future planned for her. However, her elder sister's determination and struggle to study once married was a strong influencing factor for Alisha as her family realised the potential of further study. Alisha shone at primary school, reading studiously and doing well in class. At secondary school, she exceeded her parents' expectations and therefore their friends and mentors encouraged them to send Alisha to a local grammar school. Her narrative describes a difficult transition from a very supportive secondary school to a grammar school with a 'sink or swim' attitude. Perhaps this helped prepare Alisha for the journey into tertiary education. She knew when she arrived at university that she was going to be more confident in herself, suggesting that her prior educational experiences had developed a strong resilient trait in her.

Whilst Alisha was allowed to attend university, she was expected to live at home, so she had a choice of three universities and chose the one with the course most closely aligned to her ambition. But Alisha is cognisant of the huge step change this has been for her parents. She describes her parents as illiterate who, despite their own lack of schooling, were keen for their children to succeed at school.

> So them being illiterate, they really — because it was hard for them, especially being in England where you have to read a lot. They pushed us try hard in school even though they didn't want us to go Uni, they wanted us to try hard in school. And they also — a general culture of even if you are not the best student, you do not mess around in school, you respect your teachers. And that's always stayed with me.

Unlike Surinder, Alisha found that her course was somewhat monocultural and that there were too few people around her who could reflect the values and culture that she understood; yet she too actively sought out someone that she felt was familiar.

*And then I went to [the university] and the course
seemed brilliant but there were no Asians on the
course [...] no Asians anywhere, I was just looking
round. And it was [...] because there was no — when
you're an ethnic minority and you're in a place full
of crowds, you try to find someone similar to you so
you try [...] from an ethnic minority. So, I saw this
girl who was also Asian [...] can we hang out? Yes
[...]there's no Asians here! I know. [...] looked
round and [...] there's no Asians here. So, then we
just became friends [...] because we were the same
ethnicity and we felt we were a minority.*

Alisha was also aware of the limitations of this monocultural learning environment that she found herself in. 'I like ethnic diversity because I like learning about other cultures, I find it really fascinating so I was just a bit disappointed.'

Alisha was struck by the self-segregation that she too played a part in, but she also realised that she had become more accepting of the 'white culture' at university. She no longer judged her peers for drinking and accepted their desire for a social life in a way that she hadn't previously.

*But now I'm used to it, yeah, I think I'm just more
accepting. I'm just like you go ahead and do your
thing and do what you want, I probably won't copy
you but that's fine.*

One of the striking themes in our interview with Alisha was the sense of her breaking away from her own culture and adopting that of her institution. This is not expressed as an open rejection of her family life but more a need to adapt and change to fit it.

> *I just feel like I like wearing my head scarf but when I'm wearing hijab because I look so different, I feel more unconfident and I won't be myself. Whereas when I'm wearing English clothes, I feel like I can be myself more because I feel like I'm going to be judged less for how I'm dressed. So even if I have a different viewpoint of people, I can express it, if that makes sense.*

Alisha is clear that her journey through university has made her more confident, more aware of the benefits being in a diverse classroom brings and more importantly that it has given her the choice to select the elements from her own culture that she values and leave other aspects behind. But there was a note of sadness when she describes the role that her institution has played:

> *I think because when you're in an institution there's always the culture of leave your own culture at home and get immersed in the one here. I think I've done the same [...] I do the same, I leave it, because it's always been the way it is. I leave it at home and I won't bring it to Uni and then when I'm in school, teaching, I'm still doing it, I'm still leaving my own culture at home and not bringing it into school.*

Alisha's story suggests that initially she did not feel at ease within her new university life, but that she has adapted, and shifted her own cultural identity as a result. She, like Surinder, tended initially to stay within her own cultural groupings and was disappointed that her institution did so little to encourage cultural integration.

3.5. AZIZ'S STORY

Aziz's parents are from Saudi Arabia and he and his siblings were brought up in the United Kingdom, giving Aziz a strong understanding of the UK education system. Whilst Aziz might appear not to sit within the category of second-generation migrant, he is included here as he was brought up in the United Kingdom. Aziz's choice of university and the course he studied were both determined by his parents — the university because it enabled him to look after his elder sister; the course because his parents felt that Engineering would give him good job prospects. It is clear from Aziz's narrative that coming back to the United Kingdom, after a short time in Saudi Arabia, to complete his education was important for him as he had been unable to settle in school after leaving the United Kingdom. When interviewed, Aziz was about to enter the final year of his degree programme. He expressed surprise at the open nature of his tutors and felt that this contrasted with his own cultural norms.

Like Alisha his family background and religion meant that he approached university with a number of misconceptions which were challenged during his time at university.

> Yeah, of course when you meet people from
> different countries, different backgrounds, different
> religions and different political views, you learn to
> not judge people and you learn that people do
> mistakes and that you should just learn and move
> on. You shouldn't just you know — don't judge,
> never judge people, yeah [...]

Aziz appreciated the opportunities and potential for learning that studying in a diverse classroom afforded him:

> *Yes. It's all about acceptance. This person is like this*
> *because he's like this, you can't change that. He's*
> *from that place, he has a different kind of*
> *perspective of life. You just have to accept*
> *everything and you shouldn't [...]*

But he too reflected that his institution had done very little to encourage students to benefit from the diversity of the campus: 'The only thing that the university does is it's let me meet other people but it didn't really help.' So he expressed some frustration that, whilst there was cultural diversity, there was no space either in the curriculum or more generally to acknowledge and learn from that cultural discourse.

Aziz also enjoyed the independence that university pro-vided for him – the need to think for himself and the chal-lenges that the curriculum offered. During Aziz's schooling, he experienced bullying that meant that he felt compelled to adapt to fit in. This may explain why Aziz was able to adapt and adjust and therefore feel comfortable at univer-sity. He also felt that the education provided at the univer-sity, together with the openness of staff, and the positive learning environment he had experienced had supported his journey.

Again the sense of self-efficacy and belonging were threaded through Aziz's narrative. Like Ben, he talked about the sense of fitting in and he too enjoyed the multicultural perspectives that his higher education experiences provided.

3.6. CULTURAL TRANSITIONS

What clearly emerged from these interviews was the discon-nect between home and university, echoing the findings of Thayer (2000) whose study of first-generation low

socio-economic students found the need for students to con-
tinually renegotiate between the two cultures of home and
university. Bowl (2001) goes further by highlighting the dis-
junction between the home experience and that students
encounter when entering university.

For many of these students, there was a sense that their
academic institution failed to acknowledge the cultural tapestry that they helped to create. Whilst Ben thought that this
was entirely appropriate, it is likely that his background and
strong academic grounding allowed him to transition more
easily than the other students interviewed. We have previously
proposed that universities, by ignoring the cultural make-up
of their classrooms and by failing to build on these cultural
differences, are losing out on the opportunity to enrich the
learning experiences of students (Bamford & Pollard, 2018).
As governments press higher education providers to move
towards greater widening participation, Gale and Mills
(2013) argue that there is an ever-greater onus on the institutions to create a space for those students who sit on the margins. Like those who were interviewed, Gale and Mills believe
that students add value to the diverse classrooms and that
institutions need to recognise students' strengths. They suggest
that students (and their backgrounds) should be treated as a
fantastic and exciting resource instead of universities adopting
a deficit model of their diverse student body.

Moll, Amanti, Neff, and Gonzalez (1992) go further by
suggesting that students and families with diverse life experience are a fund of historically accumulated and culturally
developed knowledge and skills that are beneficial to the individual student. By acknowledging this fund, students are
offered a sense of positivism within the university environment from which they can benefit as they adapt. Dennis,
Phinney, and Chuateco (2005) have previously argued that
students with a strong sense of self-worth are those who are

able to cope better through that transition. Academics, by acknowledging the advantages that the diversity of students bring, can enable those participating in the academic setting to develop their self-worth. Leaving the world in which they were familiar and moving into a new one that was immediately identified as a poor fit were felt by many (but not all) of the students interviewed. The way they adapted to this change and immersed themselves into this new 'culture' was important to their successful transition but, as Alisha so profoundly points out, 'you have to leave your culture at the classroom door'.

Phelan, Davidson, and Cao (1991) describe the multiple worlds that secondary school students face and the struggle they have negotiating between the different worlds. Their research led them to suggest that schools that attempt to override these barriers have a better opportunity to develop academically engaged students. What we found significant was that all the students in our interviews reflected on the positivism of such negotiation and the freedom that they gained as a result. London (1989) similarly describes the way in which students from low socio-economic background 'break away' from their home cultures as they acculturate into higher education. Ben recognises, perhaps more than the others, that the cultural diversity of the classroom allowed him to break away from the home; Aziz also expressed a sense of empowerment that he felt his university has given him.

> *Transitions can lead to profound change and be an impetus for new learning, or they can be unsettling, difficult and unproductive. Yet, while certain transitions are unsettling and difficult for some people, risk, challenge and even difficulty might also be important factors in successful transitions for others. (Ecclestone, Biesta, & Hughes, 2010, p. 2)*

Phelan et al. (1991) and Jackson and Livesey (2014) noted that students who were best equipped to transition were those who sought friends from similar backgrounds who provided mutual strong social support. We too saw this in our interviews, with both Surinder and Alisha expressing a preference for staying within the cultural groups that were familiar to them, and for Alisha, it was crucial that she found friends that she understood.

Some argue that this lack of engagement across cultural groupings can be attributed to students' choice for self-segregation, but Jackson and Livesey (2014) propose an alternative view. They suggest that students find support where there is mutual understanding. They therefore tend to create communities of support as a way to cope with the feelings of 'otherness' that higher education often creates and a way that allows them to be themselves within what is often a 'white habitus'. Our interviewees also suggested that the act of forging ties with those culturally familiar allowed students to fit in. The fact that ethnic students from Oxford were moved to express their sense of exclusion through the 'I too am Oxford' campaign (Dhungel, 2014) which sought institutional change would suggest that this sense of 'othering' does indeed occur within our universities.

Whilst students are not reluctant to cross-cultural boundaries, they start their journeys at university seeming to prefer the support of peers from similar backgrounds. However, the students we spoke to soon came to realise the benefits that contact with students from other cultures offered once they began to feel at ease within their new culture. Allan (2003) discusses 'frontier crossing' in native and non-native speakers in secondary schools and focuses on the importance of cultural dissonance in providing a means of intercultural learning. By having to navigate through cross-cultural interactions, he believes that students develop cognitive skills, empathy and self-confidence. This sense of self-realisation and determination were also themes that emerged from our interviews, exemplified by Aziz who articulated that university had helped him 'evolve'.

This resonates closely with the words of Kylie Hillman:

> *The processes by which young people come to identify with, and become members of, a study community has been compared to the stages of development as individuals evolve from youth to adult, or by which migrant peoples are enculturated into their new community: the stages of separation (from the previous group), transition (interaction with the new group), and finally incorporation or integration into the new group. (Hillman, 2005, p. 1)*

What holds students back initially may be their own cultural prejudices. Camargo and Stinebrickner (2010) believe that students' misconceptions about different races and cultures maintain the very clear groupings that can be seen in universities. Both Alisha and Aziz talked about their own misconceptions of British cultures (e.g. about alcohol use by their peers) and how university helped them to see through those misconceptions. This presents an interesting dilemma for universities attempting to build a sense of belonging and engagement. We have seen that students who have little interaction with or knowledge of their fellow students are more likely to struggle: this appears to be compounded if the values and beliefs of the academic setting are unfamiliar to them.

Another theme that emerged from the interviews was the importance their family played in supporting their educational journey. This has been previously observed: Dennis et al. (2005) found that whilst the understanding and expectations of university life held by ethnic minority first-generation students tended to be less realistic and demonstrated a lack of understanding; those who managed the transition had strong family support. As Thayer (2000) reminds us, this support is crucial for students who are the first in their families to enter university as there is little prior understanding of the expectations within this new habitus. We heard this from Farah and Alisha who had no experiences to fall back on and no family knowledge to draw upon. Both these interviewees described their sense of disappointment that their universities did not support students' cultural transition. This may in part explain why the students from more middle-class backgrounds (e.g. Ben and Parvinder) seemingly anticipate little support from their institutions.

Research suggests that the availability of such support is often a better predictor of success than academic achievement at secondary education. Dennis et al. (2005) observed that those students whose families had encouraged them to see education as the ladder to success were more likely to find ways to cope. This ties in with Alisha's comments that her family's respect for education was at the heart of her success. If family support and experience are key, and if many of our students are the first in their families to experience university, what knowledge can they draw upon?

NOTE

1. Students with parents immigrated to the United Kingdom.

CHAPTER 4

STRANGERS IN YOUR OWN LAND

Any education given by a group tends to socialize its members, but the quality and value of the socialization depends upon the habits and aims of the group.

J. Dewey (*Democracy and Education*, 1916)

Acknowledgement of the impact of socialisation within the university is clearly not new, given Dewey drew attention to the issue in 1916. However, as yet we have observed that too little attention has been given to the 'habits and aims' of culturally different groups in terms of negotiating the layers of difference. These layers create additional complexity within the context of socialisation. Given the multi-layered backgrounds of students and the prevailing institutional habitus,[1] we have witnessed and continue to witness real challenges in finding a common ground (Arkoudis et al., 2013) for that socialisation to take place.

This chapter builds on the themes presented in Chapter 3. It further explores the potential for the cultural dissonance that may arise from the cultural interactions that take place (or indeed that do not take place) in universities between peers, lecturers and the institutions. There are micro-, meso- and macro-aspects to the dissonance, and this was witnessed both implicitly and explicitly in the students' narratives of their journeys. It is acknowledged that there are habits of coexistence in the higher education classroom amongst differing cultural groups which may present barriers to students' learning, due to differences in communication patterns and to the development or lack of development of relationships with others, specifically cultural others (Bamford & Pollard, 2018). Some of the literature focuses on the theme of dissonance by framing it within a discourse of student belonging (Pokorny et al., 2017), which is applied in a context of commuter students; in other words, those students who commute to university to participate in classes and then leave again, continuing with their lives in the urban environment in which they are familiar. The commuter student approach to higher education is gaining some attention in the contemporary literature (Harper, Smith, & Davis, 2018; Thomas, 2018) and chimes with the narratives of the group of students that are the focus for this chapter. A frequently cited outcome of the 'commuter' phenomena is that there is often little engagement in the university learning community or in the social activities of the university (Thomas, 2018). The reason for this perceived lack of engagement might be that commuter students are required or encouraged to live at home; for them, participating in family life, not university life, is the normative behaviour. These students are often from second- and third-generation migrant communities which are located in urban environments. The cultural and urban norms for these students provide a familiar cultural setting that ensures an optimum possibility of transition to a higher education environment. Leaving the 'home tribe' is not expected or viewed as necessary, and this aspect of a higher education transition (living in a new environment and unfamiliar surroundings) is thus removed. However, it may result in challenges around engagement which previous work has identified (Bamford et al., 2015). For urban institutions, the issue of engagement and creating a learning community can be a particular challenge, as often students do not have the advantage of close accommodation or access to campus accommodation and so have to commute to university from their local home community. They are frequently more engaged in a social sense in their local communities, which are often ethnically centred, rather than in the university community.

The need to understand how students transition to their university environment has been the subject of a considerable body of literature and there has also been a considerable focus within institutions on initiatives to encourage engagement in university life (e.g. Kahn, 2014; Bryson, 2014). The student body may have been drawn from the local community where measures like the Indices of Multiple Depravation (IMD) indicate the extent of social deprivation amongst the student body and where the institution has a strong widening participation mission. This was the case with a couple of the institutions that students in this study attended. It appears that the cultural frames of reference with which students arrive at university present an even more complex picture in terms of enabling transition; thus, engagement and institutional lack of acknowledgement of cultural diversity can lead to dissonance. This can be seen not just in terms of a lack of belonging but potentially in non-belonging. This cultural dissonance was powerfully evident in some of the student narratives and, in others, it was more subtly expressed. Data from an engagement survey undertaken in two London institutions reinforce the lack of communication between student groups, and this has been referenced in Chapter 1, (Bamford et al., 2015). Our data from this engagement survey underlined that there is a potential lack of communication amongst students from different cultural backgrounds and thus creating a scenario where students may choose to self-select their cultural and insider groups.

The questions around cultural dissonance arose in relation to uncertainty, responsibility and relations with others. Welikala and Watkins (2008) and Killick (2015) underline the importance of understanding cultural relations in the classroom; however, the emphasis for their discussion is in relation to international students. Quite rightly there is a need for a rebalancing of the deficit model within which international students are so often discussed, as highlighted by Marginson (2014) and others. However, there is also potentially a far less visible deficit model for students who are British but with differing cultural and often lower socio-economic backgrounds. The work undertaken by Mountford-Zimdars et al. (2015) underlines the potential for differential academic achievement for students from differing cultures, and our own research has led us to believe that there is a need to focus on cultural interactions between students due to the link to differing communication patterns and frames of reference. Whilst focused on the experience of international students, Welikala and Watkins' (2008) discussion of differing communication patterns in the classroom which influence students' learning brings this issue of communication patterns, together with the effects on the classroom experience, into sharp focus. If culture is seen as the fabric of meaning for individuals (Geertz, 1973), then differences in that fabric of meaning can lead to dissonance in a situation where there is a lack of understanding of the importance of that meaning during communication between individuals.

This communication can be as simple as body language, and therefore, an understanding of cultural context is important to understanding cultural interactions. Many cultures (Hall, 1989), for example Chinese or Latin cultures, have high context modes of communication and the use of the body can lead to dissonance before a word is even uttered. This cultural communication can simply be a matter of knowing when to talk and not to talk, as outlined by Welikala and Watkins (2008). We believe that the multitude of differing cultural values and norms that students bring into the classroom requires further attention. Some of the students expressed the need to be culturally open and adapt. The following excerpt encapsulates this view:

> [...] And it's important to be different. So I try to stick to [name of friend] of Egypt, never changed, even when I went to live in France. Stick with my background, take these ideas, get in my head [...] Yes sometimes we need to be open-minded and this is what being in a different country push me to do [...] accept others ideas and even if I disagree with them [...] just accept it and yes we are still friends. In the old days when I was in Egypt − no way! If you don't believe in the way I am thinking − no way, I am gonna listen to you! (George)

This excerpt evidences movement, transition and the potential for openness and encapsulates the nature of the impact we anticipate the higher education process should have.

As we indicated in the Introduction, throughout our own time in higher education, we have been influenced by the notion of education being, in many senses, about striving to higher ideals through the educational process, together with the transformation of those individuals who participate. We believe that the institutions which deliver *higher education* should bear some responsibility in addressing this cultural difference in classrooms so that students working with each other can benefit from learning about different cultural perspectives; this includes the global and glocal perspective as well as the migrant perspective. The classroom is a place of communication and the interviews presented a picture of both barriers that were being raised and communication being broken. If communication is broken, then cultural dissonance can and does arise. In other words, higher education institutions are aware of the diversity in their classrooms,[2] which is not just as a consequence of a growing number of international students but also of the increasingly culturally heterogeneous student body. We make this rather bold statement as the literature is littered with the struggles that international students have with their cultural transitions arising from their differing cultural scripts as identified by Welikala and Watkins (2008). However, in our previous work in two post-1992 institutions (as mentioned above), we identified that from 393 respondents to a survey on engagement issued to all undergraduate students in two different faculties, 48% identified themselves as being non-native speakers of English. The difficulties and challenges arising from cultural transitions apply to both international students and students of migrant families and are marked aspect of the cultural journeys that have been given voice in this book.

4.1. MOHAMED'S STORY

Mohamed's narrative is an account of such dissonance. Mohamed gained a place at a top Russell Group institution in the Midlands to study science at undergraduate level. He comes from a middle-class Muslim family but did not see himself as particularly religious. He felt that the start to his university experience was not a good one as he was late in applying for a place in halls of residence. The institution has a reputation as a strong campus institution and provides students with a full campus life. However, Mohamed had to live off campus, commuting to university from a small village. Not only did he have to adjust to moving from the urban environment of London but his new university environment did not appear to resonate with him in cultural or social terms. He felt that he could not adjust and the unfamiliarity of his living accommodation shone a spotlight on his inability to feel part of his new learning community. Although Mohamed did not have a strong religious identity with his home community, the unfamiliar frames of reference resulted in his cultural dissonance and reinforced his sense of difference with those around him and his new environment.

> *[...] I went to two universities. The first university experience after school I went to [name of first institution attended] and I ended up dropping out in my first year. [...] Not even after one term.*

> *[...] it wasn't a good fit for me. I had problems with my accommodation and things like that so I moved from living in a city in the middle of London to basically the countryside in a very small village. So I wasn't living on the campus where I was studying, I was living on another campus in the countryside, very small, maybe 20-50 people there type village, apart from the campus. And I didn't mesh with that school, I didn't like it.*

In response to being asked why he thought this was, he outlined the reasons for his dissatisfaction with the university:

> *One, the distance; it was about a 30-40-minute bus*
> *to the campus and only shuttle bus. There wasn't*
> *any public transport; there was the university shuttle*
> *bus that you had to catch at certain times to get to*
> *the campus and if you miss it, you are stuck in one*
> *place or the other. So I would miss classes;*
> *sometimes the bus would be full. But also, it was*
> *much less multicultural than I was used to.*

Mohamed was asked to expand on the reasons for making this statement about the university not being multi-cultural:

> *Much more English people and much more middle*
> *upper class people than I had grown up with. Not*
> *that there was a problem but with everything*
> *together, I didn't make as many friends as I made in*
> *my next university.*

He was asked to consider whether he learned anything culturally from the experience that he had in the Midlands:

> *Maybe that I am more used to this multicultural*
> *way of life than I thought or more – not stuck –*
> *I don't know how to say it [...]*

He recognised that his frame of reference, which he felt he considered for the first time, was more multi-cultural than he had realised and when the familiar cultural norms and values of growing up and living in different ethnic communities were removed, his sense of discomfort was profound:

> *[...] more depending on it than I thought, maybe.*
> *I'm used to having 24-hour shops open all the time,*
> *can go eat a [...] and stuff like that, there's people*

> *around. Yeah, it's different, village life is a lot*
> *different than London life.*

When he realised that the issue was neither commuting nor the subject that he was studying, but rather that the centre of his discomfort was missing his familiar urban environment and urban culture, he decided to go to university in London even though it would he would still need to commute.

> *I commuted. First Central Line and then motorcycle*
> *or bicycle, it took me about a half hour commute.*
> *So it felt more like college to me than university,*
> *I could go there and come back.*

We explored together the notion of the London-based Russell Group University where he studied and the fact that to him it felt more like a college than a university, which he was more comfortable with and this appeared pivotal in the new-found success he had in his studies:

> *It just felt like I was going to school. Compared to*
> *how it was living and people coming to school in their*
> *pyjamas and stuff like that and it was like they were*
> *living at the school. Because [...] really a campus, [...]*
> *campus university more than most I think. A big*
> *campus, a lot of people on campus. I think there's*
> *people [...] didn't have to leave campus if they didn't*
> *want to because there's a supermarket and shops on*
> *campus and restaurants, clubs on campus.*

He gave some thought to whether his view of his experi- ence would have been different if he had been living on cam- pus at his first university:

> *I'm not sure. I kind of didn't like that. The campus*
> *and [city name] was pretty different. I went to*

different parts of London to get a haircut and stuff,
but that's a cultural thing. I went to go to an Afro
barber to get a haircut and that area is much
different than the people on campus [...] [town
where university located] has a strong Afro
Caribbean community. And the people from the
university don't really go to that part of London and
they just stick to the campus, maybe go to clubs at
the weekend.

He felt that being part of the urban environment was important to his cultural frames of reference and norms of behaviour as he felt more comfortable in coming and going to and from his higher education environment. Indeed, he preferred this learning experience to the campus experience in the Midlands where the higher education environment was the focus for all his activity. The urban environment felt comfortable but it had to be an environment that he was familiar with:

I like to feel part of the city and can go where
I want [...] I felt more comfortable. I felt more
comfortable definitely Because it was in, and out.

[...] I think I could leave when I want and come
back – I could come any time and go any time
[...] I could still go and see my friends if I wanted
and if I wanted to stay in university I could stay
in the library. I was far enough away from home
that I wasn't being distracted by friends so
I could go and no one is going to come and find
me in East London to distract me. But if I want
to come back I could come back in half an hour
quickly.

Some of our previous work has underlined the importance of friendships in university life and that these friendships are often formed early on in the course and changed little over time (Bamford & Pollard, 2018). Religious and ethnic groupings can be bridged when these friendships are formed but our previous work echoed the view expressed by Mohamed, that the institutions themselves do little to concern themselves with students' social adaption. Perhaps more attention is required to avoid early dissonance, and universities should be more aware of and should consider the differences in students' backgrounds and aid students in traversing the barriers that are identified.

4.2. THE POTENTIAL FOR CULTURAL UNDERSTANDING IN HIGHER EDUCATION

Through the students' narratives of their cultural journeys, we clearly saw that cultural adaption and acceptance were features of their experiences. Sometimes, the experiences were described only in cultural terms; in other words, the whole higher education experience can be viewed as being framed by a cultural context. This is important in the sense that it is the cultural context to the classroom and the learning environment that are so little understood or drawn on. It may be that culture should, as some students confirmed, be left at the classroom door; but in the search to understand the learning experience, some aspect of the cultural context needs to be given further attention. The importance of the cultural context is illustrated by John's story. Whilst he comes from an Anglo-Saxon background, John has been included as white working-class male students are one of the least represented ethnic groups in some universities.[3] John was someone who came from a lower socio-economic and disadvantaged background and did not know anyone else who had gone to university.

4.3. JOHN'S STORY

John's journey into higher education was rather different from other students interviewed: he had an Anglo-Saxon background and came from a low-income single-parent family with no family members having ever gone into higher education before him. After a spell in the army and working as an engineer, John returned to education. He did his English qualifications and an Access course, gained a First in his undergraduate course and completed a Master's degree. He observed that his journey had been cultural as well as educational:

> *My Access course at college, it was a really diverse group and for me, there was an English girl who had a Chinese father and it was just really interesting to see all these different walks of life, because I don't feel I'd been exposed to it in the real world you know up until that point. I mean I did have some of it in the Army but a lot of it was mainly white British guys, a couple of Fijian guys and South African but even then it was [...] because of their accents and it was kind of part of the culture.*

He felt it was important to emphasise that the experiences he had during his education were very different from those in the army, especially as the cultural interactions he had encountered at college and university had a deep and lasting impact:

> *[...] I think it's changed a lot now; I've got friends with [...]. And for me it totally changed my*

perspective on how I approached people, I think
how people approach you as well I think. I think
that's all changed.

The diverse classroom experiences that John encountered had helped him broaden his views and horizons. During the university experience, he learnt to situate the narrow views that he had been brought up with by being exposed to and interacting with those from other cultures. However, John displayed strong cultural dissonance on a university field trip to China which was required as part of his Masters course. The cultural differences in the group of students were brought to the forefront as the group interacted with each other in the foreign environment which, for John, proved difficult to adjust to:

Yeah, I think for me, I had a different view of China
and I had this idea of beautiful mountains and
bonsai trees and all that sort of thing. Maybe
seeking some herons catching some fish and all that
sort of stuff, more traditional in China. And I think
going to Beijing, I think I had like a modern view of
China but culture for me is really important in the
sense of like historical stuff. If I go somewhere I like
to check out the architecture and a bit of the history.
[...] but there was nothing of the actual sort of
people [...] in Beijing left, like the little temples and
all this sort of stuff. I felt like it had just been, had
its heart ripped out, there was just like this concrete
jungle. For me the interesting stuff was gone so it
was just like being a big dirty Western city.

I just felt that the city was dirty, obviously because
of the pollution and I think when you see a dirty
country you can't relate that to the people quite

easily. And it's not really, when you look at it,
they're just the victim of circumstances because of the
pollution and everything, because of all the factories
and stuff. But then when they're spitting on the floor
as well you find that disgusting, because the western
culture it's disgusting to do that. So when you see
someone doing it, you think yuck, but then you have
this sense of difference with that person.

The previous cosmopolitan attitude that was evidenced throughout John's narrative shifted to a display of strong cultural dissonance and evidences the sort of impact that negative cultural interactions can have in a learning environment. The field trip became a negative experience and, for John, enhanced the cultural differences in the group he travelled with.

4.4. ALISHA

Although we introduced you to Alisha in Chapter 3, we have included her in this chapter as her narrative identifies a strong sense of cultural dissonance. For her entire life, her parents, who had immigrated from Pakistan, had said she would not be allowed to go to university. She expressed this as a real disappointment to her. She had always wanted to attend university: she was influenced by her school experience, by her peers around her going off to university and by having career ambitions that fell in line with attending university first.

Both of my parents are illiterate. My [...] from
Pakistan but he didn't like school, he wasn't very
good at it. And back when he went, if you didn't
listen or you didn't [...] you got hit. If you missed
days off school, you got hit so then you just didn't
go to school. And he would rather stay at home and

*help his dad. And then he came to England when he
was 13 or 15 and his education stopped. My mum
never got to go to school in Pakistan. She's been to
English courses here and there but never really [...]
and she can read the Koran so even though she's
illiterate, she classes herself as illiterate, I don't
know as much because she can read the Koran.*

*So them being illiterate, they really — because it was
hard for them, especially being in England where
you have to read a lot. They pushed us try hard in
school even though they didn't want us to go uni,
[sic] they wanted us to try hard in school. And they
also — a general culture of even if you are not the
best student, you do not mess around in school, you
respect your teachers. And that's always stayed
with me [...]*

Alisha's parents relented with regard to her attending university after her sister's challenging experience at the Open University to become an accountant, where she had struggled with having a baby at the same time. Aisha's choice of university was based on the reputation of the institution but aligned strongly with the experience of the group we have referred to as 'commuter students', as she expressed the desire to commute from home to university:

*Because I can go to university and I can stay
at home.*

*To get here it takes me about an hour and a half so
that stops me from getting distracted and keeps me
focused because if it's a 9 o'clock start I get up at
half past six. But it takes an hour and a half to get
here so I'm gonna try [...]*

The final comment relates to her difficulties in her commute which is a theme for students who fall into the commuter student category. She refers to her transition to university:

> No one really prepared you for how independent it is. I think there [...] A levels are going to be so much more independent than your GCSEs. [...] because you will be in school [...] to get the best grades. No one really tells that at university you're going to get here and it's like 'do this', we're not going to hear much about it, go off and learn it. So that was a big transition but I like university because when I got here, I was gonna be more confident. I did wear a hijab quite a few times in the first year but I didn't feel comfortable wearing it.

She further explained that:

> Again no one else was. I just feel like I like wearing my head scarf but when I'm wearing my hijab because I look so different, I feel more unconfident and I won't be myself. Whereas when I'm wearing English clothes, I feel like I can be myself more because I feel like I'm going to be judged less for how I'm dressed. So even if I have a different viewpoint of people, I can express it, if that makes sense.

There appears to be some link expressed here between her confidence and being identified by her headscarf: that she felt safe and secure in her anonymity. She expanded further on the cultural differences that she felt were *hidden* in education:

> I think in schools in higher education, there's a culture of - regardless of what your home culture, what your home background is, you go out the door

> *and you come to school and you come to university*
> *and it's all about you leave that background at*
> *home. It's more about an English way of life and*
> *I think — because I generally have an interest in*
> *different courses, I think it's more interesting.*
> *I think it will just be nice to generally have a*
> *conversation to ask someone about things that are*
> *different. So it's kind of like [...] what's your*
> *ethnicity, if you mention something. Like they don't*
> *encourage you to talk about the things that are*
> *different in your culture.*
>
> *I think they're accepting as in we'll take you as you*
> *come. So yes, you are a Muslim, you wear a head*
> *scarf. Yes, you're black, yes, you're a Chinese and*
> *that's where it stops and [...] but we don't want to*
> *delve into [...] we just want to get on with the class,*
> *we don't want to delve into it.*

The perception of tutors and students not delving into cultural backgrounds and the question of exploring personal depth here is interesting as it is in juxtaposition to the point made about acceptance. Alisha goes further and presents a picture of understanding amongst ethnic groups that she did not encounter or feel was present in the classroom:

> *I don't think — I think I'm definitely more accepting*
> *of difference but I think ethnic minorities are always*
> *more accepting [...] but they are generally more*
> *accepting. Because they're a minority I think we're*
> *just taught that you are the minority so you have*
> *different views, they have different views, it is fine.*
> *You can all get along together. But I think I have*
> *really become more accepting. When I was in*
> *school, when you were in lower school no one could*

> *drink and stuff so that part isn't there. When I was*
> *younger, it was kind of like I was drinking, it was a*
> *bad thing. Whereas now, I kind of understand that it's*
> *a common thing, it's a common cultural thing that*
> *happens here even though I'm not going to take part.*
>
> *My values I think they're the same but I'm not very*
> *open about them. I know I have some different*
> *views and stuff but I keep them to myself, I only tell*
> *one of the Muslim girls.*

She recognises that she had different views from her fellow students but appears not to be concerned to share them; in fact, she expresses the need to maintain barriers and difference that she came to accept. This evidences a dissonance in her educational experience and cultural journey; it does not chime with the narratives of the first-generation migrants interviewed who demonstrate pride and confidence in their cultural difference. Notably, this experience of dissonance is not restricted and limited by the level of education; however, perhaps it is brought more clearly into focus in the higher education environment. This discomfort and barrier-building is clearly illustrated through her narration of a particular session that appears to have had an impact on her at many levels. The particular session was centred around Prevent Policy[4] training:

> *We had prevent training and it was in a lecture and*
> *because – and I feel like [...] I feel it's a*
> *safeguarding thing but a government policy that is*
> *created to suggest and deliver the teacher to suggest*
> *that you need to be watchful of Muslim kids and*
> *[...] Muslim kids because they are more likely to be*
> *terrorists then that says something about how the*
> *government sees those Muslim kids. They are a bit*

*of a threat. And obviously we need to tackle, they
need to tackle terrorism and radicalisation but I'm
uncomfortable with the Go Home policy that's
trying to push training [...] terrorism into school.
And when this lecture was going on, I didn't say any
of that until like the end when everyone had gone
and I was talking to the guy [...] one or two of the
people there. Because I thought that me raising up a
concern of mine would come across as well you
can't get the past the fact that you're Muslim so you
can't see what the issue is. I thought if I raised a
concern it would be seen as me not being able to get
past the fact that I'm a Muslim.*

It is worth noting that Alisha is the only interviewee who
raised the issue of the training session on the government's
Prevent Policy. However, it may just have been a question of
timing as the interview with Alisha followed shortly after the
training. However, her narrative evidences silencing and
alienation. It underlines a certain amount of separation and
reinforces the impression of distance and the difference that
this particular student felt. The presence of barriers is very
evident and provides a sharp contrast to some of the narratives in the previous chapter; whilst it may be a singular
experience relating to this particular student (and thus a situated event), it is government policy to deliver Prevent Policy
training. Other interviewees from second- and third-
generation migrant backgrounds echoed the strong tones of
alienation that surfaced in this narrative. Aisha's narrative dis-
plays three kinds of dissonance: micro-dissonance in terms of
challenges she has had to navigate on a personal level to attend
university, on a meso-level with Aisha identifying that she felt
that cultural difference is not recognised in the classrooms, and
on a macro-level with regard to her reaction and engagement

with the government's Prevent Policy. It evidences miscommunication, separation and cultural dissonance.

4.5. SAMAR

Samar was studying Arabic and Middle Eastern Studies at a Russell Group institution in the North of England. She had chosen to study Arabic and Middle Eastern Studies because she felt she wanted to be more closely in touch with her father's culture and language which she had not been taught as a child. Coming from a family where both parents work in higher education, Samar, like Ben in Chapter 3, was confident and had the cultural capital to understand and meet the expectations of higher education. She decided to understand more about her own heritage through her choice of degree, expanding on her interest in languages and cultures and influencing the potential for a future career. Her higher education study enhanced her understanding of her father's culture in ways that simply growing up in the United Kingdom did not allow her to explore:

> *Oh yes, it has because – well it's because I think the field I want to go into in the future is diplomacy or foreign office and I think given the current political climate at the moment it would be really useful to have Arabic as well as the other languages that I know. But I always felt, not out of place but when we would have family gatherings and my dad would be speaking to his family in Arabic and I wouldn't understand and have to ask them to translate, I just got fed up with it. So I just wanted to –*

She clearly expresses the strong desire to understand the Arabic half of her family. However, she also outlines that, as someone who grew up in London and who is now studying

in Morocco as part of her degree, she has a broad understanding of cultural difference and that she has a cosmopolitan outlook — again, this is a similar view to that expressed
by Ben in Chapter 3:

> *I think that helps being a Londoner because you're*
> *exposed to it every day. But it has helped obviously*
> *because my dad, [...] but in Morocco the culture is*
> *quite different but being there and having to live it*
> *every day, you do get more familiar with it. But for*
> *me it was easier than my colleagues who are*
> *British — we have some international students from*
> *Poland — it's a lot easier for me to get used to it a*
> *lot quicker and feel more comfortable than them.*

During her degree studies, she tried to maintain a cosmopolitan perspective and engagement with others but observes
that many of her peers were British; they appeared to her to
be less engaged with 'international others' and perhaps chose
the course mainly for career motivations:

> *I try and mix with the international students. I try*
> *and join a lot of societies just to keep myself busy,*
> *but surprisingly a lot of people who chose to do my*
> *course were British.*
>
> *[...] I think a lot of them want to work in politics so*
> *they think that's the best degree to have.*

She felt that studying at university opened up, on various
levels, the possibility to explore one's cultural identity. Samar
explained the ways in which she valued the chance to learn
from crossing boundaries:

> *I think especially being at uni it helps you, not to*
> *find your identity but you can experiment more and*

you can express yourself more. And especially because school is a different kind of environment but university is so big and there are so many different people and there's people that you don't know. So that helps a lot, you can explore more. And especially with the societies, that helps.

I guess because it provides different experiences and it's very inclusive. In the beginning of university, because I'd moved away from home, I was feeling quite lonely. But then once you —

It is interesting to note that she also confirmed that, even for someone who had acquired cultural capital, the transition from home life represented a huge step and the need for adjustment:

Yes, I was on the phone to my mum every day, like crying and 'oh I wanna come home'. She was like 'please don't come home!' You just have to — once you start talking to people and you have to make that first step.

This narrative offers an example of true relationality in cultural terms and represents an openness to the cultural context of the higher education environment which can expand horizons and help develop a cosmopolitan mind-set. in spite of her cosmopolitan attitude and strong cultural capital, Samar experienced dissonance when studying overseas as part of her degree, and this chimes with John's narrative.

4.6. BETH

Beth emigrated to London from Nigeria to be with her husband who was studying in the United Kingdom. She took on what she described as menial jobs to support him during his studies; later on, following a reduction in her working hours, she decided to study herself. As she had originally worked for local authorities, she began her studies in the field of health-care. Her narrative evidenced the struggles she had in terms of adjustment, her resilience and her determination to succeed, particularly after the death of her husband when she found herself facing life alone in this country. She expressed a deep sense of gratitude to her new country for the opportunities that she had been given and surprise that she did not see a similar sense of gratitude in young people. She makes a point of recognising the emphasis on skills and employability afforded by UK higher education:

> *I'm actually from Africa, specifically from Nigeria.*
> *I came to this country in 1989, [...] February [...]*
> *I came to better my life actually and since I came*
> *I have been working up to 2013. I worked for my*
> *local borough, [name] council for 16 years. And*
> *then unfortunately I was made redundant because*
> *they were trying to cut costs, the council were*
> *cutting costs and I had an option to [...] my contract*
> *used to be 36 hours in the week but it was changed*
> *to 18 hours, which I found difficult for me to cope.*
> *So I had an option to take early redundancy, or to*
> *take the 18 hours so I now decided to take early*
> *redundancy.*
>
> *That way I had the opportunity to study so*
> *I started [...]. I used to work at the Carers Inn and*
> *then I started to upgrade myself; I had my HND*
> *for two years.*
>
> *Hopefully in June I should be finishing my degree.*
> *And with my experience in this country, the country*

*has helped me a lot in terms of education, the
opportunity I had. I didn't have that opportunity in
my country. In my country the government won't
help you to, they won't pay for your school fees,
you will have to struggle to pay. And the education
system is quite different from this country, it's not as
good as because in my country you can see a
university degree [...] will not be able to function
well in that field. But this country they will help you,
they will train you that you will be effective when
you finish your training, you will be effective in
whatever you choose to do. So I could say in
comparison the education level is very high in this
country than where I come from. So I am actually
very grateful to the country.*

In response to a question about whether she felt she was a
determined person, Beth replied:

*Oh yeah, I am, I am. My life I believe in working
hard because nothing good comes free so you have
to work hard and thank God that I came, I was
working all my life. I never received any benefit,
I was working and [...] the country helped me and
I am grateful to the country.*

*Like when I first came, we have a high level of
respect for one another, like in the morning you
greet everybody, hello, how are you? But this
country it's different. You come sometimes you say
hello to people, with not even a response to that.
But when I first came I was oh − and the way we
respect, we don't call people by name, especially
people who are older than you, we don't call them
by them, you don't to respect them. But here*

I realised, because we are used to [...] I feel ashamed to call my manager by name. But when I realised that some people don't like — they want to be called by their name, their first name so I had to make an adjustment.

And with regard to the adjustments, she made to her new culture?

Yeah, at first I felt oh — I felt I was probably ignored but eventually when I realised that I am from a different culture, this is the way of life. And instead of — it doesn't mean that they don't respect — but — or calling somebody you know, it doesn't make them feel disrespected. So I had to adjust.

No, I was working, I am always working, I am not a lazy person, I don't believe in you are getting something for free. I believe in working and I thank God I have good health to do that.

We witness here the potential for dissonance as a consequence of cultural miscommunication and differing cultural scripts. Beth made an active intervention in terms of adjusting her behaviours. In response to being asked to consider how her journey might be viewed with regard to her interactions, Beth expressed that she had mixed with a lot of people from Africa and had learnt about the different cultural behaviours from her peers:

Yes, I have friends from other African countries and then, we interact. And I learn from them as well because we all come from different cultures, even though we are from the same Africa, [...] a big country, [...]we still have our culture [...].

*[...] we have different cultures, because as I love my
spicy food, some people, other countries don't like
spicy food.*

It is not uncommon for the theme of food to play a large
part in the cultural adjustments that first-generation migrants
make and is a topic also raised by international students
(Bamford, 2014). Despite this discussion of the different
culinary tastes, Beth did not consider that cultural difference
had presented a challenge to her: she accepted that it was a
matter of accepting difference and understanding that you
need to adapt and make adjustments for these differences in
cultural practices:

*I don't feel much challenge because I believe
different people have different − I try to take people
as they are, deal with people as they are because
I know we are from different backgrounds. So
people can never be the same so I try to respect
people, even though sometimes they don't agree
with what we are doing but − in my home, in my
family we are brought up to respect people, that is
the key [...] my upbringing.*

She does, however, identify that cultural difference can be
a challenge for families with children:

*The only thing I can say, the upbringing of kids.
Where I come from, the family is responsible to
bring up their kids, without the government's [...]
intervention. But here, sometimes with the culture
here, the parents really have to put their foot down
to be able to − they want to do much to bring their
kids but they are constrained. Sometimes because of
the government's intervention; not in terms of abuse*

but sometimes you want to your kids up in the rightful way. And they go out there, they learn from their friends, they become bad and they are not listening and stuff like that and you can't do much.

It's quite different in Nigeria; everybody will help to raise kids. I will say that I don't encourage abuse because when the kids do anything bad there is a way. It's not — you don't have to keep beating; you don't beat your kids to change them. There is a way you speak to them that they can change. But there, they have to beat you and talk to you, I don't believe in that beating. They are trained to respect people and to do the right thing. Because it's a disgrace, if somebody goes and shoplifts, the kids [...] their parents [...] goes and does something, or fights on the street, it brings shame.

Here, we can see Beth clearly expressing the challenge for parents accustomed to a mode of being which infuses and inculcates their approach to child rearing. The shift required to develop the new cultural self requires an unfamiliar response and perhaps even a temporary sense of helplessness in the new environment. It represents the potential for a lack of cultural engagement which may be passed on to the next generation.

4.7. CONCLUDING REMARKS

This chapter explored and gave voice to the phenomena of cultural dissonance for those students who define themselves as British but who also identify that they have cultural backgrounds and identities that are multi-layered. We have not explored the complex concept of identity in multi-cultural societies but acknowledge the importance of belonging to an individual's sense of identity. The students' complex cultural identities in the context of belonging were explored in the interviews. It seemed clear that questions surrounding their cultural identity and their transition into higher education needed to be given more attention than the literature currently offers. Appiah (2018) acknowledges the importance of understanding the ties that bind in the context of cultural identity but it has not been the aim of this work to explore the issues of identity.

As previously stated, we sought to understand the contribution that higher education makes to individuals' learning experience together with communication with each other in the context of their identified cultural identity. This was particularly interesting for those students who are defined as British by birth but who have a migrant family background, thereby entering university with multiple layers of cultural identity. John's story highlights the importance of these cultural interactions on growth, understanding and the potential sense of belonging that may be cultivated. The relationships with others are the glue that binds the experience. Developing an understanding and giving voice to some of their stories is vitally important in recognising the differences and similarities in the journeys of individuals through their higher education experience. The growth arising from the cultural interactions is linked to issues around belonging to the higher education tribe, whether that is in the classroom or within the social groups that are formed, as well as the transition that is made in order to succeed in terms in higher education. This chapter has focused on the extent to which the higher education environment creates dissonance in terms of the transition to the host educational institution/culture, whether there is a process of building cultural capital for the individual, or indeed whether the transition is simply about challenges around learning the subject of choice for each student. In other words, is another layer of cultural identity added through the cultural interactions that take place during the higher education process and, indeed, does this form part of individuals' cultural journeys?

Alisha highlighted the potential for dissonance through identities expressed in dress codes: her adoption of 'English' dress made her feel more comfortable and helped develop her sense of belonging. Perhaps this is an example of the zealousness that Henry was referring to in Chapter 1. She expressed how the education system is more about the 'English' way of life: that differences in cultural identity are not explored or are only acknowledged at the surface level. This theme of 'stranger' appeared to arise in particular for those whose cultural identity is multi-layered but who identify as British (not English), although born in England. The identification as British appears to allow for a recognition of the multi-layered aspects of their identities. This underlines the potential for dissonance, if indeed the education system is seen as recognising English values rather than incorporating the type of multi-cultural inclusive classroom promulgated by Banks (2015). It evidences little of the culturally cosmopolitan approach that is needed to encourage transition and a sense of belonging.

From the student narratives, we drew the importance of the cultural context of the higher education experience in general. Higher education is so intrinsically linked to individuals and their growth and sense of being that the removal — or lack of recognition — of the cultural context from the learning process fails to acknowledge the link of cultural background to the knowledge construction process. So much so that individuals' frames of reference are culturally steeped. The consequence of this is the potential for dissonance which can lead to a number of different results including an academic performance that fails to demonstrate (draw out?) the abilities of the student. In Chapter 5, we look at the importance of relationships which encourage a more positive learning experience and reduce the potential for dissonance.

NOTES

1. As outlined in Chapter 1, institutional habitus refers to the sense of the culturally framed pedagogy within universities.

2. In February 2019, the Office for Students published guidelines on requiring higher education providers to produce Access and Participation Plans which will set out how higher education providers will improve equality of opportunity for underrepresented groups to access, succeed in and progress from higher education (Retrieved from https://www.officeforstudents.org.uk/media/1093/ofs2018_03.pdf. Accessed on February 20, 2019).

3. 'More than half of universities in England have fewer than 5% of white working-class students in their intakes, according to researchers'. Amy Walker (2019) states that half of universities in England have fewer than 5% poor white students: the study finds white working-class are less likely to attend prestigious institutions (*The Guardian*, February 14, 2019).

4. Prevent is part of the current Government's counter-terrorism strategy stemming from the Counter-terrorism and Security Act 2015 and aims through safeguarding to prevent people becoming terrorists or supporting terrorism.

CHAPTER 5

CULTURE AND DEVELOPING RELATIONALITY IN HIGHER EDUCATION

In this chapter, we draw on research we have previously undertaken to enable us to take a holistic view of the narratives and to consider the potential impact of the students' higher education experience on their cultural journeys. This view is framed in terms of both their engagement with their studies, the barriers and challenges they encountered and, more broadly, their cultural interactions. As Kahn observes:

> *The way a student responds to uncertainty, responsibility and relations with others emerges as relevant to learning in a knowledge society. Students themselves take centre stage as we look to develop comprehensive understandings of their engagement in learning. (Kahn, 2014, p. 1016)*

This quote is taken from Kahn's theoretical positioning of student engagement in relation to a distributed agency perspective and highlights the need for a broader understanding of students' emotions, together with active participation and contribution to their higher education learning. It forms the emphasis for the focus in our work, that is giving voice to the narratives of students' experiences and cultural journeys. Each narrative provides a variation of the experience of different cultures in higher education, and this book as a whole pulls them together to present the themes that can be drawn from the students' cultural journeys. We anticipate that, by allowing for these voices to be heard, our understanding will be enriched and enhanced and that further acknowledgement of the cultural capital that students bring will be given more attention. We have argued in this book that interactions and relations with others are relevant to students' learning in the context of the cultural background that frames those relationships. These culturally defined communications relate directly to students' will to learn (Barnett, 2007). As individuals, students bring themselves into the classroom, and recognition of this agency as individual actors underpins their sense of belonging. What appears to be the overarching link is the way relationships are formed or are absent, the way these relationships are sustained and then how they inform the cultural narratives that have been the feature of this work.

In Chapter 1, we considered our previous work: the data generated by the research project funded through an Higher Education Academy (HEA) Teaching Development Grant provide further context and contribute to the themes that are identified in the previous chapters. As we state in Chapter 1, we wanted to hear more from the individuals studying in UK higher education about their lived experience and the way in which the phenomenon of individuals' cultural backgrounds formed part of their educational journey. We felt that was value in a more in-depth exploration of the students' voices with regard to their higher education experience.

This final chapter draws these themes together by acknowledging students' challenges, barriers and successes in negotiating the higher education landscape. The interviews that were undertaken to inform this study provide insights that allow educationalists to hear the voices and understand the perspectives of those with different and multi-layered cultural backgrounds and the university to allow the development of relationality between students and institutions. It evidences the need to focus on the existential parameters of higher education, recognising the potentiality of the heterogeneity of the engagement for individuals, whilst also acknowledging the challenges. Akin to Kahn's analysis (2014), we acknowledge that whilst this work does not explore the issue of identity as a factor in student engagement, cultural identity informs communication approaches and has a symbiotic relationship with engagement, thus recognising the importance of an individual's perceived cultural identity on engagement and the potential for belonging. Whilst we have touched on the issue of cultural identity because of its link to students' way of being in the classroom, our perspective is informed by Hall's view (1996) that:

> [...] identities are never unified and in late modern
> times increasingly fragmented and fractured; never
> singular but multiply constructed across different,
> often intersecting and antagonistic, discourses,
> practices and positions. They are subject to a radical
> historicization, and are constantly in the process of
> change and transformation. (2015, p. 4)

Much has been written that chimes with the above, and this book is an acknowledgement of this context for the higher education learning environment. We have witnessed from the narratives that differing cultural identities are still little understood or addressed and – as yet – continue to present a challenge.

The evidence suggests that these challenges can be addressed if the attention shifts to facilitating communication between students from different cultural backgrounds, bridging barriers and developing resilience and relationality. This would encourage greater engagement in the learning environment, rather than fostering the dissonance that arises from a lack of appreciation of different communication patterns. In essence, the ability to communicate with others, irrespective of cultural background and native language, can be seen as cosmopolitan engagement and a key feature of the higher education learning environment (Bamford & Pollard, 2018).

By revisiting the theme of 'leaving your culture' at the classroom door in Chapter 3, we can see that, when a person transitions to university and leaves who they are at the classroom door, it amounts to leaving who 'they' are, existentially outside the classroom. And yet we have witnessed that there is an expectation of engagement within the classroom on a level that is deeply personal and one that relates to an individual's shifting identity. It may seem obvious to say that individuals bring themselves into the classroom – their 'voice' is the point of communication and interaction. There is certainly a discussion to be had about learning in relation to the ontological that Barnett (2007) underlines, and the existential which requires further exploration in the context of differing cultural identities. However, it appears that there is an issue around the individual voice being ignored or disregarded: in doing so we are not appreciating students' *being* in higher education at a deeper and philosophical level as well as dismissing a potential strength to the classroom environment that is part of the educational process in which students participate. As Barnett acknowledges, 'through gaining her own voice, the student becomes herself' (2007, p. 99) where voice is a metaphor for educational ideals such as 'freedom, authenticity and becoming itself'. This leads, however, to the need to accept relationality as a concept that frames both the educational process and the cultural interactions of students. Alisha in Chapter 4 exemplifies this challenge for educationalists to consider. The underlying issue here is that we may be denuding the very education that we are seeking to deliver. In most basic analysis, this might be viewed as not allowing students to be seen as the individuals they consider themselves to be. Have universities lost sight of the potential gains that different cultures could bring to the classroom? How can academics improve their recognition of students' cultural frames of reference and cultural interactions? For example, should science academics, when teaching evolution, elicit the views of their students who may have different cultural perspectives? We have argued that increasing a sense of belonging may be key to developing habits of coexistence as well as a space where the ever-changing shifts of cultural identity facilitate the educational process to take hold and for students to flourish.

We have argued that we need to explore further student's responses to uncertainty, responsibility and relations with others, which arise from differing communication patterns. Together with our previous research, the narratives in this book complement the work of others such as Kahn (2014) who identifies that relations with others are important in understanding student engagement – a topic that is not explored within the confines of the current text but nevertheless directly links with the way in which learning takes place in higher education.

Previous studies (Bamford & Pollard, 2018; Mountford-Zimdars et al., 2015) suggest that for significant groups of students, the transmutation of the will to learn (Barnett, 2007) into an educational outcome is in doubt. In terms of a cultural perspective of this conundrum, we draw on Matthews' (2000) analysis of the cultural shaping of individuals in contemporary societies. Matthews argues that the cultural shaping of the self exists on a number of levels and cognition of the cultural self might be perceived as challenging — in other words, we can never see ourselves the way others see us — and the development of a reflexive approach to communication is something very few achieve. For Matthews, norms and rules of behaviour are defined by cultural codes. These codes are often tacit and we think in the language of our culture, which makes a reflexive perspective of our behaviour difficult to achieve. The question is then not one of knowing our cultural behaviour to allow for communication but rather reflection on how to avoid miscommunication. Clearly, poor communication may result in dissonance that does not lead to the positive frame of mind that is needed to support the 'will to learn'. The ability to reflect on our own norms of behaviour and intonations of language and movement are steeped in our cultural and social practice and can present a challenge. As confirmed by the testimonies in this book, the question remains whether the skills required to navigate the culturally plural learning environments, as well as those needed for active participation in the learning environment in higher education, have been given sufficient attention.

5.1. COSMOPOLITAN LEARNING ENVIRONMENT

The diverse classroom provides opportunities for the lived experience of cultural difference and Lee, Williams, Shaw, and Jie (2014) provide evidence that well-managed classroom interactions can increase students' confidence with their intercultural interactions. The documented unevenness in student achievement from studies, such as demonstrated by Mountford-Zimdars et al. (2015), highlights the need for universities to explore further the complexities of cultural difference within the student body and perhaps engage in a more dialogic approach to cultural difference (Bamford & Pollard, 2018; Trahar, 2011). There is evidence that institutions that adopt a learning approach that draws on students' differing cultural backgrounds to enhance the learning experience, as well as facilitating the development of transferable skills, are positioning themselves to lead the way in teaching excellence.

This leads us inexorably to considering how to frame such an approach conceptually and to promote a discussion of cosmopolitanism. Appiah (2006) underlines that cosmopolitanism is not a new concept, having its origins in Stoicism and etymologically from the Greek word *cosmopolites*, meaning a citizen of the world. The intention here is not to promote notions of the global citizen as part of the higher education curriculum but rather to focus on our common humanity and the potential for cultural learning so as to create opportunities for additional learning and the development of belonging. The space for such an approach would appear to be needed but it cannot be viewed in a one-size-fits-all approach. Institutions need to acknowledge that the cultural diversity and differing values and norms that students bring to their educational environment cannot be 'left at the door' if we are to encourage a true *higher* learning environment. Banks (2015) outlines the need for developing praxis around the cultural plurality in the classroom environment, recognising that there has been a failure within higher education institutions to embed an approach that encourages equality of opportunity of different groups. He refers to academic acknowledgement that multiculturalism has failed in UK and German institutions. The discourse from scholars in both these countries suggests that this has arisen from a failure of the implementation of a multicultural approach in secondary education in neither policy or practice. Our research supports that this lack of multicultural approach remains true.

We take the view that a way forward in understanding the impact of the culturally heterogeneous make-up of the higher education student body would be to adopt a cosmopolitan approach to communication between cultural others so that the classroom can provide a relational dynamic to the learning experience. The higher education environment offers a natural forum for differences in communication patterns to be incorporated into the learning construct. Appiah (2018) challenges us to address the difficult task of shifting cultural identities and living with cultural complexity. Our student voices have evidenced the nature of this complexity in higher education classrooms and underlined the need for our common humanity in our teaching and learning approaches; rather than restrict it, this would allow for our sense of ourselves, as shaped by countless affiliations, to contribute to the higher education process.

A construct of cosmopolitanism that allows for a frame of our common humanity to be promulgated as a basis for classroom communication creates a space for learning that enhances students' belonging. In other words, this incorporates the approach that Arkoudis et al. (2013) propose as a basis for an effective learning environment where a common ground for interactions is sought. It offers the opportunity for educational success to those who come from differing cultural backgrounds. Banks (2016) outlines a model of differing variables, typologies and conceptual schemes that are required for a functioning model of multicultural education to be developed. He conceptualises US school education as needing to be formulated around five dimensions: content integration, knowledge of the construction process, prejudice reduction, empowering school, social structure and an equity pedagogy.

We have not adopted these dimensions to analyse the student responses, but there is certain synergy with Bank's dimensions and the overwhelming evidence of the need to provide a more culturally inclusive approach to higher education. The complexity of the cultural experience for students demands that universities facilitate a learning experience that chimes more comfortably with their expectations and understanding of self that they bring to the classroom.

Rizvi acknowledges the importance of offering students a 'mode of learning about, and ethically engaging with, new social formations' (2009, p. 254), thus contextualising in learning terms the global shifts in migration that have come to be represented in higher education classrooms. These global shifts are represented as physical embodiments of cultural difference that demand engagement both between teachers/students and between students/students. As yet, there appears to be little recognition of the multiple layers of identity that the globalised environment has brought to the forefront of the learning experience. Kahn (2014) and Trowler (2015) recognise that there is a need for variation at the level of the individual in the education process. In part, this often singular approach to teaching can be odds with the multiple cultural identities that students bring with them when entering university: it would be difficult, however, to create an environment that suits this heterogeneity. Our students' narratives reinforce the notion that an acknowledgement and understanding of the influences on students' active participation in culturally diverse higher education classrooms are needed. These influences are steeped in cultural norms and values which stem from the students' cultural and social backgrounds. Our evidence, as voiced by the students, demonstrates the students' wish for their experiences and their 'persona' to be appreciated, rather than be left at the door or acculturated into an environment that limits their transformation through a *higher* education. It seems that, although we acknowledge these differences, there has been little change to the environment in terms of pedagogy or 'habitus' of higher education institutions. Those who do not arrive with the cultural capital to engage with the format of delivery of *higher* education appear to find the challenges and barriers more difficult to overcome. From the stories that we heard, these challenges have caused students to leave their universities and seek institutions where they felt they could belong.

5.2. THE IMPORTANCE OF RELATIONSHIPS

As we have observed, a common theme that emerged from the data was the importance of relationships which allowed individuals to develop agency through engaging with others from different cultural groups. These relationships appear to build confidence and are transactional in the sense that a positive context to engagement allows for building blocks or layers of agency for each party to develop. An example of the importance of the development of agency is offered by Maria:

> *Mm, I love it! It is one of the reasons I am in London! Because I love diversity, I love to interact with other group! Saying that, I see some people, you know: they don't like to interact with another group. So, you see for example, one ethnicity group with another, one group with another and then [...] the odd ones (laughing). I'm the odd one - the Latino group, you know. You move from one group to another. But, honestly, Germans, they stick with the Germans. And if you do an assignment with the*

> *German people they will speak with you in German*
> *(laughing). Because I remember, I did an assignment*
> *with the Germans and they would only speak*
> *German. And I would speak German by the end of*
> *the assignment (laughing), you know, because [...]*
> *'Yeah, yeah, I agree with you. Ya, ya!' Because some*
> *people, you know, but I think [...] Because me,*
> *I believe you have to mix, interact with everyone,*
> *because otherwise you miss out! So I try to get*
> *involved with everyone. I don't care. You know,*
> *sometime I just come to the group, they sit there [...]*
> *You know. But, saying that, it is quite divided.*
> *People would only stick to their own ethnicity*
> *I found out...which I don't like. I like people mixing*
> *with each other. Because we would learn more from*
> *each other. If we actually spent more time talking*
> *with each other. We can resolve so many issues just*
> *by talking with each other [...].*

There is a reflexive aspect to this narrative that is not always witnessed in students' recounting of their cultural journeys: it perhaps reinforces the difference in confidence levels of those who are first-generation migrants as Maria is. Even when recounting the negative, there is a positivity in the tone and recognition that knowledge could be acquired through a relational paradigm with other students being a source of learning. Maria acknowledged not only the importance of communication, differing communication patterns and the potential disruption to learning as a consequence of cultural barriers but also that cooperation with others can be a facet of the learning environment and that cultural barriers needed to be crossed. Maria's narrative was not unique in its acknowledgement that others could be a source of learning: but this excerpt offers one of the clearest examples of what appears to be a thread of recognition by students of a commonality based on each person's common humanity. It is this sense of humanity which forms the basis for a cosmopolitan framework for encouraging student engagement. Maria refers to herself as the 'odd one', underlining her separation from the German students to whom she refers. There is also an appreciation that the cosmopolitan environment of London generates the potential for cultural fluencies, which this student views as part of her education. This was echoed very strongly in Parvinder and Ben's narratives.

5.3. BARRIERS TO *HIGHER* LEARNING

Our students' stories evidence that there are barriers to being and belonging in higher education that appear to arise due to the shifting cultural identities of the student body. However, the cause of the barriers is not fully understood and certainly the opinion that it is a student-driven issue may imply either some sort of deficit model of cultural identity or that the challenge of transitioning to being a higher education student is due, to some extent, to a lack of effort on the part of a student. The cultural identity issue must be viewed as a two-way street, and the perceived intransience of institutions to acknowledge the need for culturally steeped change as part of the transition can be seen as contributing to the barriers encountered. Thomas (2002) lays the suggested inadequacies in performance and attainment from certain groups at the door of the institutions that provide higher education that the issue may be the prevailing and persistent institutional habitus. From our narratives, we can see that these barriers are not insurmountable but there is clearly a difficulty in transition which is threaded throughout the students' accounts. The rarefied language of higher education and the communication styles of lectures offer an example of the ways in which institutional habitus can create cultural dissonance for students, and the dissonance witnessed in some narratives can be attributed to apparent differences in communication styles from lecturers and from the administrative centres in universities. Observations undertaken in previous research supported this attribution of barriers and the importance of peer group support (Bamford et al., 2015). Distance, in the sense of remoteness from tutors — and perhaps even exposure to the unknown and unfamiliar that universities represent — requires the development of resilience and persistence skills in order to navigate some of the most basic aspects of university life. As we have highlighted above and in previous chapters, a feature of overcoming barriers appears to be the development of relationships which carry individuals through their higher learning experience. These relationships are formed early on in the students' higher education life cycle and are maintained after university. They can be with peers or tutors but the importance of such relationships to the development of persistence and resilience cannot be underestimated.

Informal networks and communities were features of students' coping mechanisms to develop and thrive in what for some initially seemed a hostile environment. A lack of community was also clearly expressed to be a barrier. For those who were confident and academically successful, an established community was an important aspect of their success with positive references being made to their networks either formal or informal. The absence of a community appears to reinforce the distancing effect and results in the dissonance that we focused on in Chapter 4. This dissonance underlines the importance of creating and developing a wider learning community. For the students who told their stories, a community was important and a feature that students felt universities should facilitate. However, in urban environments, we have witnessed that some students found their peers' focus on travelling into university and departing quickly made it difficult to for them to cope with university studies as it did not allow for a community and for relationships to develop. The challenge of the 'commuting' student was discussed in Chapter 4, and it presents an additional barrier for institutions in urban environments.

It appears that there is also a question around pedagogic approach which hinders students' engagement with learning. The search for high-impact solutions (Evans, Mujis, & Tomlinson, 2015) to pedagogic approaches has received a lot of attention and yet, for certain groups, the challenge remains. Our conviction is that the barrier remains in place because there is a need for culturally responsive approaches to culturally plural classrooms. We need to be clear here in stating our opinion that it is not that lecturers do not demonstrate awareness of the cultural plurality of the classroom, but rather that there perhaps is insufficient attention given to the effects on the classroom experience of students' differing cultural backgrounds. This is not a decolonisation of the curriculum discussion, but rather that a discussion of differing communication patterns requires some attention. Again, Banks (2016) supports this need for a shift in pedagogy in terms of an embedded approach to cultural difference. Gay (2000) defines 'culturally responsive teaching' as an approach that uses cultural knowledge, prior experiences and the performance styles of diverse students to make learning more appropriate and effective for them. Students form friendships early on during their courses and engage with each other's cultural differences but their institutions appear to do little to consider different ways in which contrasting ethnic and religious backgrounds may impact on the students' ability to communicate with each other. An example here is religion.

British universities recognise religious difference amongst their student communities but do little to adapt or embrace how this might inform a world view. As we saw in Chapters 3 and 4, this has resulted in an impression for some students that they must leave their culture at the classroom door. This might impact on the 'will to learn' identified by Barnett (2007) and goes to the very heart of individual's *being* in higher education.

5.4. BRIDGING BARRIERS AND LISTENING TO THE STUDENT VOICE

Nixon (2012) asserts that awareness of the complexity of the human condition can lead to a sense of powerlessness for individuals and thereafter a loss of agency:

> *A major consequence of the plurality of the human condition is the impossibility of fully comprehending the outcomes of our own and others' actions — the extent to which the ways in which our myriad actions interconnect and interrelate. (Nixon, 2012, p. 109)*

He identifies that once there is a realisation of the complexity of the human condition, the only way to counter and confront the potential polarising of reactions (either the need for control or a sense of powerlessness) is through modes of understanding that develop 'mutuality and reciprocity of human agency.' (2013, p. 109). We have attempted throughout this book to address the impact of the plurality of the human condition through the twin themes of developing understanding and relationality. This focus on building understanding is important in the context of encouraging the will to learn (Barnett, 2007) to which we have previously made reference. The educational experience needs to encourage engagement and the enthusiasm that the will to learn represents rather than allowing cultural dissonance to be paramount: educators need to create an environment where the challenges to communication with others are overcome. The narratives reinforced that the will to learn is a fundamental dynamic of the learning process. The powerlessness and loss of agency alluded to by Nixon (2012) was witnessed in the stories that our students told of their higher education experiences. Nixon further observes:

> *Learning individualizes us and enables us to become ourselves through the clarification of our interests and the development of our particular aptitudes and capabilities. Education can either acknowledge the individualized dynamic of human understanding and thereby focus on individual self-development and flourishing, or it can insist upon conformity and homogeneity and in doing so restrain and restrict that dynamic. (2012, p. 117)*

The higher education establishment should be seen as playing an important role in securing the ability to develop an understanding of the way cultural difference feeds into and forms part of the learning process: that relationality and mutuality between individuals allow for the possibility of a cosmopolitanism engagement by students who bring their multiple layers of cultural identity to their learning environment. The ability to understand the difference, and the tools needed to develop relationality between groups, points to the need for institutions to consider focusing on building the undergraduate community in a more concrete way, thus permitting the development of agency.

As we have seen, the need for cosmopolitan engagement is promulgated around a notion that students need to develop the skills to bridge barriers with different cultural groupings in order to negotiate the university environment. The risks are lack of engagement and poor performance for certain identified groups. This is now commonly referred to in the literature as differential attainment but which needs to be linked to the identification of the performance of different cultural groups. This view regarding the importance of the development of agency through a relational dynamic to the learning environment is echoed in Mountford-Zimdars et al.'s work (2015): that enhancing communication, together with the social and cultural cohesion between peer groups, appears to enhance student belonging and thus student outcomes.

Adding further weight to the proposition that there is a need to contextualise engagement within a frame of cosmopolitanism is the link between engagement and outcomes for students from diverse ethnic backgrounds. Kezar's (2014) supports a focus on the development of social networks which enable the flow of knowledge across the rigid boundaries imposed by the curriculum. The importance of boundary crossing for the enrichment of knowledge is supported by the work of Akkerman and Bakker (2011). Crossing the rigid boundaries allows students to collectively take the risk of changing their academic behaviours. However, this needs to be sustained. The danger, as Handley, Sturdy, Fincham, and Clark (2006) found, is that people can quickly revert back to their culturally familiar groupings. The challenges around this form of risk-taking need to be recognised and addressed pedagogically if we are to have any hope of pushing the current boundaries to engagement in a culturally pluralistic society.

5.5. CONCLUDING REMARKS

The purpose of this book has been to provide an opportunity to students who come from differing cultural backgrounds the opportunity to tell their 'story'. The interpretation of their stories is inevitably limited by being situated in terms of time and space that is dependent on individuals' particular views of their experiences at the time they chose to portray them. However, we observed common themes arising in the narratives that chimed with our previous work and our own experiences of talking to students during our many years as educators in higher education institutions. The complexity of cultural identity represents a limitation in being able to convey any generalised position – and no doubt we will continue to try to understand how such complexities feed into the learning process and knowledge acquisition for individuals. This does not mean, however, that an attempt to argue the need for change should not be made, nor that the issue of cultural negotiation and the development of a relational dynamic to the *higher* learning process should not be attempted, or even that there should be a fundamental rethink of the way in which we deliver our higher education.

We found that students from different cultural backgrounds appear motivated to engage at university but there is a lack of relationality amongst different groups, which we suggest affects their sense of belonging. Those who come from first-generation migrant backgrounds displayed different levels of confidence in 'who they are' and this confidence overflows into their 'will to learn' and into their ability to engage with cultural others. This confidence was also displayed with those who came from more cosmopolitan second-generation backgrounds, whose family backgrounds had enabled them to transition to university as a result of the cultural capital they had acquired. The stories evidence that institutions need to do more to understand the ways in which the cultural make-up of their student bodies impact on students' engagement with their studies and that there is a need to facilitate students' relationality in order to enhance learning. The sense of separation that was referred to by some was not common to all. However, from the perspective of delivering an impactful pedagogical approach, the evidence points to the widespread effect of such separation for certain groups which has the potential to influence performance. Universities continue to acknowledge the cultural plurality of their student body but appear unable or unwilling to change the nature of the delivery to an approach that is cosmopolitan and is not dependent on the cultural capital with which students come to university.

The importance of high-impact pedagogies that use 'real-world' examples and simulations enabled stronger communication between students in this study and has been highlighted by Evans et al. (2015) and Bamford et al. (2014) as an effective approach to engaging students. Cosmopolitan engagement should therefore be viewed as a high-impact pedagogical approach to the learning environment. There is a need to focus on the development of community and encourage cosmopolitan engagement and communication across different cultural groups.

This work has sought to highlight the current inconsistencies that exist and give voice to the students' perspectives of those inconsistencies. The claim is that the curriculum should be informed by the student experience in a more concrete manner than the way we currently deliver it and this change will contribute to a more rewarding and enriching educational experience. This framing of higher education in a more personalised way is something which some institutions are beginning to recognise, for example, the Nottingham Trent University Personalisation Project.[1] In other words, moving forwards, institutions need to begin to address the effects of the impersonal which we observed in students' narratives. We saw this discomfort with the impersonal clearly in some of the narratives, particularly in the stories of Farah, Parvinder and Alisha. The need for belonging is not a call for homogeneity but instead a recognition that the educational experience should be personalised. Confidence also has a role to play in success: this confidence appears to be derived either from a personal assuredness in cultural identity and maturity or from socio-economic background. Once that confidence develops, we witness the tone of the students' stories changes with evidence of flourishing and excelling. This flourishing does not appear to be grounded necessarily in aptitude[2] but often reflects the resilience that students develop. The standing of the university did not appear to influence the ability to flourish; in fact, for some, it was a hindrance with the dominant factor being the individuals' qualities which were identified, for example, the ability to communicate with and be comfortable with others. The narratives can be seen as cultural journeys and these cultural journeys evidence transformations. A lack of transformation results in alienation and dissonance. Higher education is relational and personal because of these transformations that occur, and those of us working in higher education need to do more to assist students so that they can flourish and achieve the results they deserve.

NOTES

1. https://www4.ntu.ac.uk/nbs/document_uploads/193068.pdf

2. Entry qualifications were not discussed but a presumption of entry to higher education was taken as the basis for the ability for further development.

BIBLIOGRAPHY

Abolghasemi, A., & Varaniyab, T. S. (2010). Resilience and perceived stress: Predictors of life satisfaction in the students of success and failure. *Procedia Social and Behavioral Sciences*, 5, 748–752.

Akkerman, S. F., & Bakker, A. (2011). Learning at the boundary: An introduction. *International Journal of Educational Research*, 50(1), 1–5.

Allan, M. (2003). Frontier crossings: Cultural dissonance, intercultural learning and the multicultural personality. *Journal of Research in International Education*, 2(1), 83–110.

Al-Sharideh, K. A., & Goe, W. R. (1998). Ethnic communities within the university: An examination of factors influencing the personal adjustment of international students. *Research in Higher Education*, 39(6), 699–725.

Appiah, K. A. (2006). *Cosmopolitanism: Ethics in a world of strangers*. London: Allen Lane.

Appiah, K. A. (2018). *The lies that bind: Rethinking identity*. London: Profile Books.

Arkoudis, S., Watty, K., Baik, C., Yu, X., Borland, H., Chang, S., & Pearce, A. (2013). Finding common ground: Enhancing interaction between domestic. *International Students in Higher Education*, 18, 222–235.

Bamford, D. N. (2010). *Person, deification and re-cognition: A comparative study of person in the byzantine and pratyabhijna tradtitions*. Unpublished Thesis, University of Chichester, West Sussex, England.

Bamford, J., Djebbour, Y., & Pollard, L. (2014). Does subject matter, matter? A comparison of student engagement in culturally diverse classrooms in urban, cosmopolitan higher education institutions. *Investigations in University Teaching and Learning*, 9, 26–35.

Bamford, J., Djebbour, Y., & Pollard, L. (2015). 'I'll do this no matter if i have to fight the world!': Resilience as a learning outcome in urban universities. *Journal for Multicultural Education*, 9(3), 140–158.

Bamford, J. K. (2014). *Dealing with difference: Developing an understanding of international postgraduate joint degree programmes in business in London and France*. Unpublished PhD Thesis, Institute of Education, University of London, United Kingdom.

Bamford, J., & Pollard, L. (2018). Developing relationality and student belonging: The need for building cosmopolitan engagement in undergraduate communities. *London Review of Education*, 16(2), 214–227.

Banks, J. A. (2015). *Cultural diversity and education*. New York, NY: Routledge.

Barnett, R. (2007). *A will to learn: Being a student in an age of uncertainty*. Maidenhead: Open University Press.

Barthes, R. (1993). *The semiotic challenge*. Oxford: Basil Blackwell.

Bates, M., & Miles-Johnson, T. (2010). *First year student resilience as a factor in retention and engagement*. Working

Paper, School of Criminology and Criminal Justice, Griffith University, Brisbane. Retrieved from https://eprints.soton.ac. uk/397472/1/Bates%2520%2526%2520Miles-Johnson% 252C%25202010.pdf. Accessed October 23, 2017.

Benhabib, S. (2002). *The claims of culture: Equality and diversity in the global era*. Princeton, NJ: Princeton University Press.

Berry, J. W., & Ward, C. (2006). Commentary on 'redefining interactions across cultures and organizations'. *Group & Organization Management*, *31*(1), 64–77.

Blythe Liu, L., Baker, L., & Milman, N. (2014). Technological innovation in twenty-first century multicultural teacher preparation. *Journal for Multicultural Education*, *8*, 54–67.

Bowl, M. (2001). Experiencing the barriers: Non-traditional students entering higher education. *Research Papers in Education*, *16*(2), 141–160.

British Educational Research Association. (2011). *British educational research association ethical guidelines*. British Educational Research Association. Retrieved from http:// www.bera.ac.uk/wp-content/uploads/2014/02/BERA-Ethical-Guidelines-2011.pdf. Accessed on October 23, 2017.

Bryson, C. (Ed.) (2014). *Understanding and developing student engagement*. New York, NY: Routledge.

Burns, J. (2017). 'Sharp rise' in student mental illness tests universities. *BBC News*. Retrieved from https://www.bbc.co.uk/ news/education-41148704. Accessed on December 10, 2017.

Buttny, R. (1999). Discursive constructions of racial boundaries and self-segregation on campus. *Journal of Language and Social Psychology*, *18*(3), 247–268.

Camargo, B. R., & Stinebrickner, T. (2010). Interracial friendships in college. *Journal of Labor Economics*, *28*(4), 861–892.

Caruana, V. (2014). Re-thinking global citizenship in higher education: From cosmopolitanism and international mobility to cosmopolitanisation, resilience and resilient thinking. *Higher Education Quarterly*, *68*(1), 85–104.

Cassidy, S. (2015). Resilience building in students: The role of academic self-efficacy. *Frontiers in Psychology*, *6*, 1781.

Cherng, H., Turney, K., & Kao, G. (2014). Less socially engaged? Participation in friendship and extracurricular activities among racial/ethnic minority and immigrant adolescents. *Teachers College Record*, *116*(3), 1–28.

Chiswick, B. R., & DebBurman, N. (2004). Educational attainment: Analysis by immigrant generation. *Economics of Education Review*, *23*(4), 361–379.

Chung, E. D., & Chur-Hansen Turnbull, A. (2017). Differences in resilience between 'traditional' and 'non-traditional' university students. *Active Learning in Higher Education*, *18*(1), 77–87.

Clandinin, D., & Caine, V. (2008). *Narrative inquiry*. In L. M. Given (Ed.), *The Sage encyclopaedia of qualitative research methods* (pp. 542–545). Thousand Oaks, CA: Sage Publications.

Clandinin, D. J., & Huber, M. (2005). Shifting stories to live by. In D. Beijaard, P. Meijer, G. Morine-Dershimer, & H. Tillema (Eds.) *Teacher professional development in changing conditions* (pp. 43–59). Dordrecht: Springer.

Cox, B. E., & Orehovec, E. (2007). Faculty-student interaction outside of class: A typology from a residential college. *The Review of Higher Education, 30*(4), 343–362.

Crawford, C. (2014). *Socio-economic differences in university outcomes in the UK: Drop-out, degree completion and degree class.* Working paper no. W14/31, IFS Working Papers.

Crisp, G. A., Taggart, A., & Nora, A. (2015). Undergraduate Latina/o students: A systematic review of research identifying factors contributing to academic success outcomes. *Review of Educational Research, 85*(2), 249–274.

Cross, M., & Atinde, V. (2015). The pedagogy of the marginalized: Understanding how historically disadvantaged students negotiate their epistemic access in a diverse university environment. *The Review of Education, Pedagogy, and Cultural Studies, 37*, 308–325.

Dennis, J. M., Phinney, J. S., & Chuateco, L. I. (2005). The role of motivation, parental support, and peer support in the academic success of ethnic minority first-generation college students. *Journal of College Student Development, 46*(3), 223–236.

Dent, S. (2017). Introduction. In *Collaboration, communities and competition*. In S. Dent, L. Lane, & T. Strike, (Eds). *International perspectives from the academy* (pp. 93–106). Rotterdam: Sense Publishers.

Dewey, J. (1916). *Democracy and education: An introduction to the philosophy of education.* New York, NY: MacMillan Publishers.

DhungeI, B. (2014). I too, am Oxford: The intricacies of racism today. *The Independent* [online] Wednesday, March 19.

Retrieved from https://www.independent.co.uk/voices/
comment/i-too-am-oxford-the-intricacies-of-racism-today-
9200337.html. Accessed on March 22, 2019.

Dronkers, J., & Fleischmann, F. (2010). The educational
attainment of second generation immigrants from different
countries of origin in the EU member-states. In J. Dronkers
(Ed.), *Quality and inequality of education* (pp. 163–204).
Netherlands: Springer.

Duckworth, A. L., Peterson, C., Matthews, M. D., & Kelly,
D. R. (2007). Grit: Perseverance and passion for long-term
goals. *Journal of Personality and Social Psychology*, *92*(6),
1087.

Ecclestone, K., Biesta, G., & Hughes, M. (2010). Transitions
in the lifecourse. In K. Ecclestone, G. Biesta, & M. Hughes
(Eds.), *Transitions and learning through the lifecourse*
(pp. 1–15). London, Routledge.

Estebana, M. P. S., & Martía, A. S. (2014). Beyond
compulsory schooling: Resilience and academic success of
immigrant youth. *Procedia Social and Behavioral Sciences*,
132, 19–24.

Evans, C., Mujis, D., & Tomlinson, D. (2015). *Engaged
student learning: High impact strategies to enhance student
achievement*. York: Higher Education Academy.

Gale, T., & Mills, C. (2013). Creating spaces in higher
education for marginalised Australians: Principles for socially
inclusive pedagogies. *Enhancing Learning in the Social
Sciences*, *5*(2), 7–19.

Gale, T., & Parker, S. (2014). Navigating change: A typology
of student transition in higher education. *Studies in Higher
Education*, *39*(5), 734–753.

Gay, G. (2000). *Culturally responsive teaching: Theory, research and practice*. New York, NY: Teachers College Press.

Geertz, C. (1973). *The interpretation of cultures*. New York, NY: Basic Books.

Gibbs, G. (2010). *Dimensions of quality*.York, UK Higher Education Academy. Retrieved from https://www.heacademy. ac.uk/system/files/Dimensions_of_Quality.pdf. Accessed on June 19, 2016.

Glass, C. R., & Westmont, C. M. (2014). Comparative effects of belongingness on the academic success and cross-cultural interactions of domestic and international students. *International Journal of Intercultural Relations*, *38*, 106–119.

Goodenow, C. (1993). Classroom belonging among early adolescent students: Relationships to motivation and achievement. *The Journal of Early Adolescence*, *13*(1), 21–43.

Goodson, I., & Sikes, P. (2001). *Life history research in educational settings: Learning from lives (doing qualitative research in educational settings)*. Buckingham: Open University Press.

Grayson, J. P. (2008). The experiences and outcomes of domestic and international students at four Canadian universities. *Higher Education Research & Development*, *27*(3), 215–230.

Grosseck, G., Bran, R., & Tiru, L. (2011). Dear teacher, what should I write on my wall? A case study on academic uses of Facebook. *Procedia-Social and Behavioral Sciences*, *15*, 1425–1430.

Gunawardena, C. N., Hermans, M. B., Sanchez, D., Richmond, C., Bohley, M., & Tuttle, R., (2009).

A theoretical framework for building online communities of practice with social networking tools. *Educational Media International*, 46(1), 3–16.

Gunnestad, A. (2006). Resilience in a cross-cultural perspective: How resilience is generated in different cultures. *Journal of Intercultural Communication*, 11, 1.

Gunnestad, A., Larsen, A., & Nguluka, S. (2010). Resilience in minorities. *Journal of Intercultural Communication*, 22. Retrieved from http://www.immi.se/intercultural/nr22/ gunnestad-22.pdf. Accessed on October 23, 2017.

Gurin, P., Dey, E., Hurtado, S., & Gurin, G. (2002). Diversity and higher education: Theory and impact on educational outcomes. *Harvard Educational Review*, 72(3), 330–367.

Hall, E. T. (1989). *Beyond culture*. New York, NY: Anchor.

Hall, S. (1996). Introduction: Who needs 'identity'? In S. Hall & P. du Gay (Eds.), *Questions of cultural identity* (pp. 1–17). London: Sage Publications.

Handley, K., Sturdy, A., Fincham, R., & Clark, T. (2006). Within and beyond communities of practice: Making sense of learning through participation, identity and practice. *Journal of Management Studies*, 43(3), 641–653.

Hargittai, E. (2007). Whose space? Differences among users and non-users of social network sites. *Journal of Computer-Mediated Communication*, 13(1), 276–297.

Harper, S. R., Smith, E. J., & Davis III, C. H. (2018). A critical race case analysis of Black undergraduate student success at an urban university. *Urban Education*, 53(1), 3–25.

Hassim, T. C., & Strydom, H. (2013). Resilience in a group of first-year psychosocial science students at the North-West

University (Potchefstroom Campus). *West East Journal of Social Sciences*, *2*(1), 40−46.

Hausmann, L. R., Schofield, J. W., & Woods, R. L.. (2007). Sense of belonging as a predictor of intentions to persist among African American and White first-year college students. *Research in higher education*, *48*(7), 803−839.

HEFCE. (2014). *Differences in degree outcomes: Key findings*. Issues Paper no. 2014/03. Retrieved from https://dera.ioe.ac.uk/19811/1/HEFCE2014_03.pdf. Accessed January 28, 2019.

HESA. (2014). *Higher education statistics*. Retrieved from https://www.hesa.ac.uk/stats

HESA. (2017). Retrieved from https://www.hesa.ac.uk/data-and-analysis/students/whos-in-he/characteristics

HESA. (2018). Higher education statistics 2016/17 [online]. Retrieved from https://www.hesa.ac.uk/news/11-01-2018/sfr247-higher-education-student-statistics. Accessed January 28, 2019.

Hillman, K. (2005). The first year experience: The transition from secondary school to university and TAFE in Australia. *LSAY Research Reports*, 44.

Holley, D., Volpe, G., & Kane, S. (2014). My first ideal day: Implications for induction from a three (London) university project. *Networks*, *17*(1), 87−95.

Jackson, A., & Livesey, K. (2014). Enriching the student experience: Engaging students and staff. In C. Burson (Ed.), *Understanding and developing student engagement* (pp. 238−250). London: Routledge.

Jones, S. (2017). Expectation vs experience: Might transition gaps predict undergraduate students' outcome gaps? *Journal of Further and Higher Education*, *42*(7), 908−921.

Jovchelovitch, S., & Bauer, M. W. (2000). *Narrative interviewing[online]*. LSE Research Online, London. Retrieved from http://eprints.lse.ac.uk/2633. Accessed on December 16, 2018.

Junco, R. (2012). The relationship between frequency of Facebook use, participation in Facebook activities, and student engagement. *Computers & Education*, *58*(1), 162–171.

Jury, M., Smeding, A., Stephens, N. M., Nelson, J. E., Aelenei, C., & Darnon, C. (2017). The experience of low-SES students in higher education: Psychological barriers to success and interventions to reduce social-class inequality. *Journal of Social Issues*, *73*(1), 23–41.

Kahn, P. E. (2014). Theorising student engagement in higher education. *British Educational Research Journal*, *40*(6), 1005–1018.

Kahu, E. R. (2013). Framing student engagement in higher education. *Studies in Higher Education*, *38*, 758–773.

Kasworm, C. E. (2008). Emotional challenges of adult learners in higher education. *New Directions for Adult and Continuing Education*, *120*(1), 27–34.

Kezar, A., (2014). Higher education change and social networks: A review of research. *The Journal of Higher Education*, *85*(1), 91–125.

Killick, D. (2015). *Developing the global student: Higher education in an era of globalization*. Abingdon: Routledge.

Knight, J. (2004). Internationalization remodelled: Definition, approaches, and rationales. *Journal of Studies in International Education*, *8*(1), 5–31.

Lam, W. S. E. (2006). Culture and learning in the context of globalization: Research directions. *Review of Research in Education*, *30*(1), 213–237.

Lave, J. (1993). The practice of learning. In J. Lave & S. Chaiklin (Eds.), *Understanding practice: Perspectives on activity and context*. Cambridge: Cambridge University Press.

Lave, J., & Wenger, E. (1991). *Situated learning: Legitimate peripheral participation*. Cambridge: Cambridge University Press.

Lee, A., Williams, R. D., Shaw, M. A., & Jie, Y. (2014). First-year students' perspectives on intercultural learning. *Teaching in Higher Education*, *19*(5), 543–554.

Lehmann, W. (2007). 'I just didn't feel like i fit in': The role of habitus in university dropout decisions. *The Canadian Journal of Higher Education Revue*, *37*(2), 89–110.

Lewis, K. L., Stout, J. G., Pollock, S. J., Finkelstein, N. D., & Ito, T. A. (2016). Fitting in or opting out: A review of key social-psychological factors influencing a sense of belonging for women in physics. *Physical Review Physics Education Research*, *12*(2), 020110.

Liebenberg, L., Ungar, M., & Vijver, F. V. D. (2012). Validation of the child and youth resilience measure-28 (CYRM-28) among Canadian youth. *Research on Social Work Practice*, *22*(2), 219–226.

London, H. B. (1989). Breaking away: A study of first-generation college students and their families. *American Journal of Education*, *97*(2), 144–170.

Luthar, S. S. (2006). Resilience in development: A synthesis of research across five decades. In D. Cicchetti, & D. J.

Cohen (Eds.), *Developmental psychopathology* (2nd ed). Hoboken, NJ: Wiley.

Marginson, S. (2014). Student self-formation in international education. *Journal of Studies in International Education*, *18*(1), 6–22.

Masika, R., & Jones, J. (2016). Building student belonging and engagement: Insights into higher education students' experiences of participating and learning together. *Teaching in Higher Education*, *21*(2), 138–150.

Matthews, G. (2000). *Global culture/individual identity: Searching for home in the cultural supermarket*. London: Routledge.

Mayer, A., & Puller, S. L. (2008). The old boy (and girl) network: Social network formation on university campuses. *Journal of Public Economics*, *92*(1–2), 329–347.

McNamee, S. J., & Faulkner, G. L. (2001). The international exchange experience and the social construction of meaning. *Journal of Studies in International Education*, *5*(1), 64–78.

Meeuwisse, M.,Born, S. E., & Severiens, M. P. (2010). Learning environment, interaction, sense of belonging and study success in ethnically diverse student groups. *Research in Higher Education*, *51*(6), 528–545.

Miller, M. (2016). *BME attainment gap literature review*. Retrieved from https://www.sheffield.ac.uk/polopoly_fs/1.661523.

Mills, J. (2015). Can social competence be taught to older children and young adults? *BERA Blog [Online]*. Retrieved from https://www.bera.ac.uk/blog/can-social-competence-be-taught-to-older-children-and-young-adults. Accessed on July 15, 2016.

Moll, L. C., Amanti, C., Neff, D., & Gonzalez, N. (1992). Funds of knowledge for teaching: Using a qualitative approach to connect homes and classrooms. *Theory into Practice*, *31*(2), 132–141.

Morales, E. E. (2014). Learning from success: How original research on academic resilience informs what college faculty can do to increase the retention of low socioeconomic status students. *International Journal of Higher Education*, *3*(3), 92.

Mountford-Zimdars, A. K., Sanders, J., Jones, S., Sabri, D., & Moore, J. (2015). *Causes of differences in student outcomes*. Higher Education Funding Council for England, United Kingdom.

Mountford-Zimdars, A., Sanders, J., Moore, J., Sabri, D., Jones, S., & Higham, L. (2017). What can universities do to support all their students to progress successfully throughout their time at university? *Perspectives: Policy and Practice in Higher Education*, *21*, 101–110.

National Survey of Student Engagement. (2013). Retrieved from http://nsse.iub.edu/html/about.cfm. Accessed on May 12, 2013.

Newman, L., & Dale, A. (2005). Network structure, diversity, and proactive resilience building: A response to Tompkins and Adger. *Ecology and Society*, *10*(1), 2.

Nixon, J. (2012). *Interpretive pedagogies for higher education: Arendt, Berger, Said, Nussbaum and their legacies*. London: Bloomsbury Publishing.

Osterman, K. F. (2000). Students' need for belonging in the school community. *Review of Educational Research*, *70*(3), 323–367.

Pelletier, C. (2009). Games and learning: What's the connection? *International Journal of Learning and Media*, *1*(1), 83–101.

Phelan, P., Davidson, A. L., & Cao, H. T. (1991). *Students'
multiple worlds: Negotiating the boundaries of family, peer,
and school cultures*. Stanford Center, CA: Stanford
University.

Pike, G. R., & Kuh, G. D. (2005). First-and second-
generation college students: A comparison of their
engagement and intellectual development. *The Journal of
Higher Education*, 76(3), 276–300.

Pokorny, H., Holley, D., & Kane, S. (2017). Commuting,
transitions and belonging: The experiences of students living
at home in their first year at university. *Higher Education*,
74(3), 543–558.

Pring, R. (2004). *The philosophy of education*. London:
Continuum.

Read, B., Archer, L., & Leathwood, C. (2003). Challenging
cultures? Student conceptions of 'belonging' and 'isolation' at
a post-1992 university. *Studies in Higher Education*, 28,
261–277.

Reay, D. (2004). 'It's all becoming a habitus': Beyond the
habitual use of habitus in educational research. *British
Journal of Sociology of Education*, 25(4), 431–444.

Reich, J. W., Zautra, A. J., & Hall, J. S. (Eds.) (2010).
Handbook of adult resilience. New York, NY: Guilford Press.

Ritchie, J., Spencer, L., & O'connor, W. (2003). Carrying
out qualitative analysis. In J.Ritchie & J. Lewis (Eds.),
Qualitative research practice. London: Sage Publications.

Rizvi, F. (2009). Towards cosmopolitan learning. *Discourse:
Studies in the cultural politics of education*, 30(3), 253–268.

Rowntree, M. R., Zufferey, C., & King, S. (2016). I don't
just want to do it for myself: Diverse perspectives on being

successful at university by social work students who speak english as an additional language. *Social Work Education*, 35(4), 387–401.

Said, E. W. (2004). *Humanism and democratic criticism*. New York, NY: Columbia University Press.

Selwyn, N. (2009). Faceworking: Exploring students' education-related use of Facebook. *Learning, Media and Technology*, 34(2), 157–174.

Shah, S. (2004). The researcher/interviewer in an intercultural context: A social intruder! *British Educational Research Journal*, 30(4), 549–575.

Smith, S. D., Salaway, G., & Caruso, J. B. (2009). *The ECAR study of undergraduate students and information technology* (pp. 1–130), Research report, Educause Centre for Analysis and Research.

Soria, K. M., & Stebleton, M. J. (2013). Social capital, academic engagement, and sense of belonging among working-class college students. *College Student Affairs Journal*, 31(2), 139.

Thayer, P. B. (2000). Retention of students from first-generation and low-income backgrounds. *The Journal of the Council for Opportunity in Education*. Retrieved from https://eric.ed.gov/?id=ED446633. Accessed January 28, 2019.

The Guardian. (2014). *10 years of social networking in numbers*. Retrieved from http://www.theguardian.com/news/datablog/2014/feb/04/facebook-in-numbers-statistics

Thomas, L. (2002). Student retention in higher education: The role of institutional habitus. *Journal of Education Policy*, 17(4), 423–442.

Thomas, L. (2012). *Building student engagement and belonging in higher education at a time of change.* London: Paul Hamlyn Foundation.

Thomas, L. (2018). *I use my time more wisely...the implications for learning and teaching in higher education of more commuter students.* Retrieved from https://repository. edgehill.ac.uk/10453/1/Valencia%20template-commuter% 20students-revised.pdf. Accessed on November 12, 2018.

Tinto, V. (1987). *Leaving college: Rethinking the causes and cures of student attrition. University of Chicago.* Chicago, IL: Chicago Press.

Tompkins, E., & Adger, W. (2004). Does adaptive management of natural resources enhance resilience to climate change? *Ecology and Society, 9*(2), 10–23.

Trahar, S. (2011). *Developing cultural capability in international higher education: A Narrative inquiry.* Abingdon: Routledge.

Trowler, V. (2010). *Student engagement literature review.* York: Higher Education Academy.

Trowler, V. (2015). Negotiating contestations and 'chaotic conceptions': Engaging 'non-traditional' students in higher education. *Higher Education Quarterly, 69*(3), 295–310.

U.C.A.S. (2017). *UCAS undergraduate entry reports by sex, area background, and ethnic group.* Retrieved from https:// www.ucas.com/data-and-analysis/undergraduate-statistics-and-reports/ucas-undergraduate-reports-sex-area-background-and-ethnic-group/2017-entry-ucas-undergraduate-reports-sex-area-background-and-ethnic-group. Accessed January 28, 2019.

Universities U.K. (2014). *Trends in undergraduate recruitment*. London, Universities UK. Retrieved from https://www.universitiesuk.ac.uk/policy-and-analysis/reports/Documents/2014/trends-in-undergraduate-recruitment.pdf. Accessed January 28, 2019.

Vaccaro, A., Newman, M., & Daly-Cano, B. M. (2015). A sense of belonging among college students with disabilities: An emergent theoretical model. *Journal of College Student Development*, 56(7), 670–686.

Wakeford, J. (2017). It's time for universities to put student mental health first. *The Guardian Online*, September 7.

Wang, M. C., Walberg, G. D., & Haertel, H. J. (1994). Educational resilience in inner cities. In M. C. Wang & E. W. Gordon (Eds.), *Educational resilience in inner-city America: Challenges and prospects* (pp. 45–72). New York, NY: Routledge.

Wang, R. (2008). *Reading paper in Facebook*. *INFOSYS 732*. Research Paper, University of Auckland, Auckland.

Wang, R., Urquhart, C., Hardman, P., & Scown, J. (2012). Tapping the educational potential of Facebook: Guidelines for use in higher education. *Education and Information Technologies*, 19(1), 21–39.

Watkins, K. E., & Cseh, M. (2009). Competence development in the United States of America: Limiting expectations or unleashing global capacities. In K. Illeris (Ed.), *Competence development* (pp. 16–40). London: Routledge.

Welikala, T., & Watkins, C. (2008). *Improving intercultural experience: Responding to cultural scripts for learning in UK higher education.* London: Institute of Education, University of London.

Wenger, E. (1998). *Communities of practice: Learning, meaning and identity.* Cambridge: Cambridge University Press.

Wilks, S. (2008). Resilience amid academic stress: The moderating impact of social support among social work students. *Advances in Social Work*, *9*(2), 106–125.

Yorke, M. (2016). The development and initial use of a survey of student 'belongingness', engagement and self-confidence in UK higher education. *Assessment & Evaluation in Higher Education*, *41*(1), 154–166.

Zepke, N., & Leach, L. (2005). Integration and adaptation: Approaches to the student retention and achievement puzzle. *Active Learning in Higher Education*, *6*, 46–59.

INDEX

Academic confidence, 64
Academic progression,
    15–16
Academic resilience, 15
Academics, 70–71
Academic tutor, 15–16
Acceptable behaviour, 4
Acculturation, 28–29
Adaption and transition,
    45–46
Alienation and dissonance,
    123–124
Anglo-Saxon model, 51
Authenticity, 108–109

BAME (Black, Asian and
    Minority Ethnic)
    student, 28–29
Barriers to higher learning,
    116–119
Becoming and belonging,
    47
Becoming itself, 108–109
Belonging, 17–19, 61
    becoming and, 47
    and detachment, 29–30
    and identity, 37–39
    self-efficacy and, 69

Black, Asian and Minority
    Ethnic (BAME)
    student, 4–5, 28–29
Bridging barriers
    belonging, 17–19
    institutions support,
        19–24
    resiliency, 12–17
British Education Research
    Association (BERA)
    guidelines, 9

Caring responsibilities, 23
Class-cultural
    discontinuities, 5–6
Cognitive skills, 72–73
Communication, 1
    and acceptance, 14–15
    patterns, 75–77, 109,
        115–116, 118–119
Community activities, 17
'Commuter' phenomena,
    75–77
'Commuter students',
    89–90
Confidence, 123–124
Construction process
    knowledge, 112–113

Content integration,
112–113
Coping skills, 12–14
Cosmopolitanism, 59–60,
111–113
attitude, 88
engagement, 121, 123
mind-set, 96, 103
Cross-cultural
communication, 23–24
Cultural adaptation, 21
and acceptance, 85–86
Cultural barriers, 51,
115–116
Cultural behaviours,
99–100
Cultural capital, 19–20,
50–51, 96, 102–103,
105–106, 122–123
Cultural classroom, 3–6
Cultural complexity, 112
Cultural context, 85–86
Cultural differences, 15,
21, 29–30, 34–36,
49–50, 90–91,
94–95, 100–101,
110–111
Cultural dislodgment, 34
Cultural dissonance, 23,
28–29, 78–79,
87–89, 101–102,
119–120
Cultural diverse
classrooms, 49–50
Cultural diversity, 1,
61–62, 69, 71–72
Cultural dynamics, 50
Cultural engagement, 101

Cultural groupings, 72
Cultural identification,
60–61
Cultural identity, 17, 30,
33–34, 61, 67,
101–103, 116–117,
122
and achievement, 25
Cultural integration and
music, 41–42
Cultural interactions, 8,
78–79, 86–87
Cultural journeys, 26–27
and obstacles, 44–47
and transitions, 31–44
Cultural knowledge, 17
Cultural learning,
111–112
Culturally defined
framework, 5–6
Culturally plural learning
environments, 109–110
Culturally responsive
teaching, 118–119
Cultural meaning-making,
27
Cultural
miscommunication,
99–100
Cultural plurality, 111–112
Cultural realities, 58–59
Cultural resistance, 47
Cultural scripts, 27, 79–80
Cultural shaping of
individuals, 109–110
Cultural transitions,
20–21, 40–41,
69–74, 79–80

Cultural understanding in
    higher education,
    85–86
Culture
  definition, 3–4
  and developing
    relationality
    barriers to higher
    learning, 116–119
    bridging barriers and
    student voice,
    119–121
    cosmopolitan learning
    environment,
    110–114
    cultural identity, 107
    relationships, 114–116
    student engagement,
    105–106

Determination, 72–73
  and resilience, 34–36
Differential attainment,
    121
Dissonance, 92–93,
    102–103, 117–118
  alienation and, 123–124
  cultural, 23, 28–29,
    78–79, 87–89,
    101–102, 119–120
  types, 93–94

Education
  learning experience, 26
  resilience, 20–21
Educational experience and
    cultural journey,
    92–93

Empathy, 72–73
Empowering school,
    112–113
Empowerment, 71–72
Encourage engagement,
    22–23
Enthusiasm, 33–34
Equity pedagogy,
    112–113
Ethnic minority, 73–74
  students, 18
External network factors,
    16

Fascination in cultures,
    57–58
'Feeling university', 5–6,
    49–50, 51
Freedom, 108–109

Generation migrant
    communities,
    75–77
The Guardian newspaper,
    14

'Habitus' of higher
    education institutions,
    113–114
Heterogeneity,
    113–114
Higher education
  culture, 5–6
  environment, 84–85
Higher Education
    Academy (HEA), 2–3
Higher education
    institution (HEI), 2–3

'Home' student
    population, 11–12
'Home tribe', 75–77
Human capital and
    resilience, 46
Humanity, 115–116
Human social behaviour,
    17–18

Identified cultural identity,
    102–103
Identity and belonging,
    37–39
Immigrants, 20
Indices of Multiple
    Depravation (IMD),
    77–78
Individuals' abilities and
    skills, 17
Informal networks and
    communities,
    117–118
Institutional habitus,
    18–19
Integration/acculturation, 20
Intercultural interactions,
    110–111
Intercultural learning,
    72–73
International mobility,
    45–46
International Students,
    26–27
'I too am Oxford'
    campaign, 72

Knowledge enrichment,
    121

Learning
    community, 75–77
    potential, 68–69
    and resilience, 36–37
    socio-cultural theories of,
    21
'Learning from lives', 6–7
Linguistic ability, 57–58

Macro level dissonance,
    93–94
Meso level dissonance,
    93–94
Methodology, 6–9
Micro dissonance, 93–94
Migrants, 26–27
Migration and resilience,
    45–46
Miscommunication,
    109–110
Monocultural learning
    environment, 66
Motivators for learning,
    52–53
Multicultural education,
    112–113
Multicultural experience,
    59
Multiculturalism, 59,
    111–112

Narrative, 7
    inquiry, 7, 9
National Survey on
    Student Engagement
    (NSSE)
    engagement items from,
    13–14

Nottingham Trent University Personalisation Project, 123–124
Nurturing a culture, 18

Passion, 33–34
Pedagogy, 113–114
Perception and memory, 8–9
Persistence and motivation, 51
Personal challenges, 56–57
Personal engagement and resilience, 29–30
Positivism, 70–71
Powerlessness, 119
Prejudice reduction, 112–113
Prevent Policy, 92–94
Project-based learning, 14–15
Pseudonyms, 9

Reception and resistance, 30
Relationality, 16
Religious and ethnic groupings, 85
Religious identity, 80–82
Resilience, 14–15, 16–17
  and adjustment, 34–36
  and coping, 56–57
  definition, 45–46

development, 30–31
levels, 30–31
migration and, 45–46
and perseverance, 56–57
and support, 17
Resilience-based model, 17
Resiliency, 12–17

Self-alienation, 60–61
Self-confidence, 72–73
Self-efficacy, 12–14, 52–53
  and belonging, 69
Self-learnt knowledge, 58–59
Self-realisation, 55, 72–73
Self-segregation, 72
Self-worth, 70–71
Sense of positivism, 70–71
Sense of resourcefulness, 12–14
Social activities, 75–77
Social and cultural capital, 52
Social capital, 5–6, 61
Social competence, 14–15
Social interactions, 17, 20–21, 27
Socialisation, 75
Social structure, 112–113
Stoicism, 111–112
Story-telling, 6–7
Stress, 15
Struggling alone, 40

Students'
  cultural journeys,
    105–106
  engagement, 109
  resilience, 30–31
  satisfaction, 14
  social adaption, 85

Themes and narratives,
  27–28
Transitions in cultural
  terms, 27–28

University
  experience, 27–28
  learning community,
    75–77
  support, 40
Unstructured in-depth
  interviews, 8
US National Survey on
  Student Engagement
  (NSSE), 11–12

'White culture', 66

Printed in the United States
By Bookmasters